T0347397

Defensible Policies

Developing and Implementing Valid Policies for Problem-Oriented Policing

Second Edition

Defensible Policies

Developing and Implementing Valid Policies for Problem-Oriented Policing

Second Edition

Raymond W. Beach, Jr.
James S. O'Leary

CRC Press
Taylor & Francis Group
Boca Raton   London   New York

CRC Press is an imprint of the
Taylor & Francis Group, an informa business

Credits

Development Editor: M. Katherine Brown

Cover design and interior art: Jane Kleinschmidt

10   9   8   7   6   5   4   3   2   1

First Published by Lawrence Erlbaum Associates, Inc., Publishers
10 Industrial Avenue
Mahwah, New Jersey 07430

Reprinted 2010 by CRC Press
CRC Press
6000 Broken Sound Parkway, NW
Suite 300, Boca Raton, FL 33487
270 Madison Avenue
New York, NY 10016
2 Park Square, Milton Park
Abingdon, Oxon OX14 4RN, UK

ISBN 978-0-97271-343-6

Dedications

To **Joy**, **Bryan** and **Bobby**, with love and gratitude for your understanding and encouragement.

—Raymond W. Beach, Jr.

To **Oona** and **Eileen**.

—James S. O'Leary

Acknowledgements

The authors and the publisher wish to acknowledge the outstanding contribution made by **M. Katherine Brown**, the Development Editor for this project. Kit helped the authors say what they wanted to say and led the work on the production tasks that greatly facilitated getting this book into print.

In addition, the authors and the publisher thank the **Michigan Municipal League** for permission to use the sample Use of Force policy found in Chapter 5 and the policy process and sample Post-Force Reporting policy found in Appendix A. Specifically, we wish to thank the following individuals for their assistance with these policies:

- **Kevin C. Murphy**, Associate MML Director & Director of Risk Management Services

- **Gene King**, MML LEAF Coordinator, Meadowbrook Insurance Group

About the Authors

Raymond W. Beach, Jr. is the Executive Director of the Michigan Commission on Law Enforcement Standards, a Division of the Michigan Department of State Police. He has over 25 years of experience in law enforcement that includes service in the states of Michigan and Florida. Mr. Beach is a nationally recognized expert and consultant on criminal justice matters and has written and lectured extensively on police policy and procedures as well as on the use of force. He is also a co-author of *Emergency Vehicle Operations: A Line Officer's Guide, Second Edition.*

Mr. Beach has received appointments to several state and national committees/boards and is currently the chairman of the Michigan DARE Advisory Board. He remains very active in his community by regularly volunteering in support of public education, charities, and youth athletics. Mr. Beach presently holds active memberships in several professional organizations including the International Association of Directors of Law Enforcement Standards and Training (IADLEST), where he serves on the Executive Board.

In 30 years of practicing law, **James S. O'Leary, J.D.** has tried over 150 civil cases, primarily jury trials. He is highly experienced in defending personal injury lawsuits, and in particular, personal injury lawsuits resulting from motor vehicle accidents. Along with his trial practice, Mr. O'Leary acts as an arbitrator and facilitator in negligence and insurance cases. He is also a national speaker on police policy and procedure. He has written articles on premises and product liability, as well as writing extensively about police procedures and the US Constitution.

Mr. O'Leary has been a member of the American Board of Trial Advocates, the Michigan State Bar Association, the Ingham County Bar Association, and the Litigation Section of the ABA. He is currently with the law firm of Johnson & Wyngaarten, P.C, in Okemos, Michigan.

Preface

There is a belief that law enforcement policies are required simply because they help protect agencies from lawsuits in today's litigious society. Think again.

The Federal Bureau of Investigation (FBI) conducted a study involving face-to-face interviews with people in state and federal penitentiaries who had murdered law enforcement officers. The results were chilling. In every instance, the officer was murdered because he or she engaged in some type of activity that caused the perpetrator to believe the officer was vulnerable and could be killed. The acts were as simple as approaching a stopped car from the front or turning their backs instead of facing the person who had been apprehended.

These murderers are not rocket scientists. None of them even considered the consequences of their actions, such as "If I kill this officer, will I be able to get away?" They lived for the moment and acted in the moment. In their minds, the officers confronting them were not other human beings with lives to live; they were targets. Based on this study, it was concluded that it is highly probably that most officers killed in the line of duty would be alive today if they had just followed routine procedures. These are the same procedures that are established by the development, implementation, and enforcement of sound, defensible policies.

When law enforcement agencies have policies, their officers go home at the end of their shifts. When law enforcement agencies have policies, their officers have full careers, retire, and get their pensions. When law enforcement agencies have policies, their officers live to see their grandchildren.

It's that simple.

Contents

One

Need for Policy

Objectives

In this chapter, you will learn the following:

- *Policy foundation laid out by the U.S. Constitution*
- *Effect of 42 U.S.C. 1983*
- *Role of law enforcement in society*
- *Role of policies in a law enforcement agency*
- *Importance of documentation*

The United States has been called "The Great Melting Pot", but it really isn't. The continuity of America does not rest on people from many different ancestries and ethnic origins blending into one homogeneous group. The continuity of America rests on the ability of diverse groups of citizens to be part of the whole, while still retaining their rights and identities as individuals. While some actions must be restricted so that society can function in an orderly manner, every person within the United States still has the guarantee of personal security and individual liberty. It is this key component of American life that requires valid policies to be part of every law enforcement agency.

Foundation of the U.S. Constitution

Any discussion of policy begins with the United States Constitution. The Constitution was approved by convention on September 17, 1787. The first 10 amendments, making up the Bill of Rights, were adopted on December 15, 1791. These amendments guarantee individual rights in the face of contrary social demands, protecting among other things the freedom of speech, freedom of religion, the protection against unreasonable searches and seizures, and the right to due process of law before being denied life, liberty, or property.

However, the Bill of Rights did not apply to the states in any form until the late 1860s. Before that, the ten amendments only applied on a national level. In other words, states could ignore the rights granted to individuals by the Constitution. That changed with the ratification of the Fourteenth Amendment on July 28, 1868, which created the basis for constitutional rights to be applied to government at all levels.

Civil Rights Statute 42 USC 1983

Congress also created a series of civil rights statutes to help enforce the Fourteenth Amendment. For law enforcement, the crucial statute is 42 U.S.C. 1983, also known as Section 1983. It states that "every person who, under color of any statute, ordinance, regulation, custom, or usage, of any State or Territory, subjects, or causes to be subjected, any citizen of the United States or other person within the jurisdiction thereof to the deprivation of any rights, privileges, or immunities secured by the Constitution and laws, shall be liable to the party injured in an action at law, suit in equity, or other proper proceedings for redress." In plain language, Section 1983 established a form of liability in favor of people who have been deprived of rights, privileges, and immunity secured to them by the Constitution and by federal statutes.

Before Section 1983 was enacted in 1871, people could not sue state officials or people acting under state law for monetary damages in federal court. Congress created this statute because it feared that, while people could sue in state court, the state court might not provide protection for federal rights. It is important to note that this fear of adequate protection in state court is an actual instruction given to juries in 1983 actions. These are powerful words and set the tone for the righteousness of the plaintiff to be in court.

Bill of Rights

The Bill of Rights is comprised of the first 10 amendments to the US Constitution.

Amendment I

Congress shall make no law respecting an establishment of religion, or prohibiting the free exercise thereof; or abridging the freedom of speech, or of the press; or the right of the people peaceably to assemble, and to petition the government for a redress of grievances.

Amendment II

A well regulated militia, being necessary to the security of a free state, the right of the people to keep and bear arms, shall not be infringed.

Amendment III

No soldier shall, in time of peace be quartered in any house, without the consent of the owner, nor in time of war, but in a manner to be prescribed by law.

Amendment IV

The right of the people to be secure in their persons, houses, papers, and effects, against unreasonable searches and seizures, shall not be violated, and no warrants shall issue, but upon probable cause, supported by oath or affirmation, and particularly describing the place to be searched, and the persons or things to be seized.

Amendment V

No person shall be held to answer for a capital, or otherwise infamous crime, unless on a presentment or indictment of a grand jury, except in cases arising in the land or naval forces, or in the militia, when in actual service in time of war or public danger; nor shall any person be subject for the same offense to be twice put in jeopardy of life or limb; nor shall be compelled in any criminal case to be a witness against himself, nor be deprived of life, liberty, or property, without due process of law; nor shall private property be taken for public use, without just compensation.

Amendment VI

In all criminal prosecutions, the accused shall enjoy the right to a speedy and public trial, by an impartial jury of the state and district wherein the crime shall have been committed, which district shall have been previously ascertained by law, and to be informed of the nature and cause of the accusation; to be confronted with the witnesses against him; to have compulsory process for obtaining witnesses in his favor, and to have the assistance of counsel for his defense.

Amendment VII

In suits at common law, where the value in controversy shall exceed twenty dollars, the right of trial by jury shall be preserved, and no fact tried by a jury, shall be otherwise reexamined in any court of the United States, than according to the rules of the common law.

Amendment VIII

Excessive bail shall not be required, nor excessive fines imposed, nor cruel and unusual punishments inflicted.

Amendment IX

The enumeration in the Constitution, of certain rights, shall not be construed to deny or disparage others retained by the people.

Amendment X

The powers not delegated to the United States by the Constitution, nor prohibited by it to the states, are reserved to the states respectively, or to the people.

While individuals have had the right to seek redress in federal court for over 120 years, historically, the courts narrowly interpreted Section 1983, and plaintiffs rarely used it. Now, however, virtually everyone recognizes this right of redress. As such, Section 1983 has become the section of the code directly involved in citizen lawsuits against law enforcement officers and agencies. It also provides the legal underpinning for the requirement that all law enforcement agencies have policies. (See Appendix A for sample policies and processes used by the Michigan Municipal League.)

Role of Law Enforcement and Policy

Indeed, the rights of individuals have been of the highest concern since this government came into existence. As a result, law enforcement is often caught between these individual rights and the demands of society. Society wants its police agencies to control crime. However, to enforce the laws, officers must infringe on the actions of individuals who have a number of rights, not the least of which is the presumption of innocence.

Undoubtedly, more claims of alleged violation of constitutional rights are filed against law enforcement agencies than against any other governmental entity. This perception could lead one to conclude that such lawsuits prevent officers from doing the job they are sworn to do. However, this is not true. The number of cases filed against officers and agencies simply reflects a basic reality: No other government entity has more direct contact with the public. Given our strong history of constitutional and statutory protection for the individual, administrators and officers should not be surprised that the court tends to protect an individual's rights and to keep them paramount.

A striking example of this protection occurred in Chicago. In some housing projects, children were being killed in the cross-fire of gang wars over the control of drug trade. The situation was desperate and called for desperate measures. The Chicago Police Department began massive warrantless searches of project buildings, confiscating the guns they found. This police action was welcomed by the citizens who lived in these projects and who were subject to the searches. However, when challenged in court, the judge ordered the searches stopped, and found them to be in violation of the Fourth Amendment. All individuals, even those who may be ruthless drug dealers and responsible for the deaths of children, have the right to be secure against warrantless searches and seizures.

In response to this emphasis on individual rights, some agencies have developed an "us versus them" mentality. When this attitude is taken, a message is telegraphed to officers that justice occurs only through their own individual action. An officer comes to believe it is up to him or her to make decisions that are reserved by law for the courts. The result is a system of physical abuse, perjury, violence, and ultimately, disrespect for the very rights and system of justice an officer is sworn to uphold.

Instead of the counterproductive "us versus them" mindset, an agency should take a higher view. As stated earlier, the single element holding the United States together is the recognition by each individual in the country that the Constitution applies to him or her. An agency should adopt the position that its officers are the foot soldiers of the Constitution, bridging the gap between the needs of society and the rights of individuals. The only way to do this is through policies. Policies guide officers, putting into words, and eventually into action, the means by which an agency and community interact.

It is important to understand, however, that while the Constitution applies to all people within the United States, no model policy exists that can be applied throughout the country. Communities are different, not just from state to state, but often from county to county. Different communities will require different methods of responding to a given situation.

The actions of law enforcement officers must have the tacit approval of the community that they serve. As such, the policies developed to guide those actions must have that approval, as well. Developing policies that meet the needs of society while protecting the rights of individuals is a challenging task. The remaining chapters of this book are designed to help you accomplish that goal.

Importance of Documentation

The importance of documenting the entire review and development process cannot be overemphasized. A policy states an agency's position, but it does not show how that position was reached. By documenting the process, you can demonstrate the following background information:

- Why the policy was necessary

- What you hoped to accomplish by developing a policy

- How you accomplished your goals

With a well-documented process, you can show that you were not reactive or just borrowing someone else's policy. You can prove that you took the time to consider the needs of the agency, of the community, and of the officers who use the policy to guide their daily activities.

In addition, accurate documentation further increases a claim of reasonableness on your part. If your process or policy is ever questioned, anyone can look at the file to understand how you reached your conclusions. They may not agree with those conclusions, but you do not have to prove agreement. You just have to prove that you were reasonable. Without documentation supporting your position, your process of policy development is open to wide interpretation and criticism.

Good documentation is also critical from a historical perspective because the people who make the policy decisions may not be available to defend them if the policies are challenged. This happens frequently in law enforcement because of the almost constant personnel movement that occurs with transfers, promotions, and retirements. If the process is documented, the agency always has access to the information that led to specific decisions.

Discussion Questions

1. What is the crucial Civil Rights statute when it comes to law enforcement? How does it create a need for policies?

2. What are the dual responsibilities of law enforcement officers and agencies? How do those responsibilities conflict, placing law enforcement in the middle?

3. Why are there more claims of alleged constitutional rights violations filed against law enforcement agencies than any other public entity?

4. How do policies establish law enforcement officers as foot soldiers of the U.S. Constitution?

5. Why is it imperative that all aspects of policy review and development be accurately documented?

Notes

Two

Three Cases Affecting Policy

Objectives

In this chapter, you will learn the following:

- *Policy implications of Monell v. Dept. of Social Services of the City of New York*
- *Policy implications of Canton v. Harris*
- *Policy implications of Tennessee v. Garner*

Every law enforcement officer in the country knows the implications of the word "Miranda". The Supreme Court decision in the Miranda case was a simple one. For the Fifth Amendment right against self-incrimination to be effective, individuals in custody must be told they have the right to counsel before being interrogated about their suspected involvement in a criminal offense. Mr. Miranda was arrested and charged with kidnapping and rape. He was not informed of his right to counsel, and confessed to a crime without the assistance of an attorney. His conviction was overturned. This situation gave rise to the Miranda warning, which affects the way in which all law enforcement officers operate.

Few cases have Miranda implications and very few need to be known by name. However, in the context of policies, you need to be familiar with the three cases discussed here.

Monell v. Dept. of Social Services of the City of New York

The first case, *Monell v. Dept. of Social Services of the City of New York*, 436 U.S. 658 (1978), was decided by the Supreme Court in 1978. This case involved a policy of New

York City's Department of Social Services and Board of Education that required pregnant employees to take unpaid leaves of absence before those leaves were medically necessary. The employees brought a class action under 42 U.S.C. 1983.

As stated in the previous chapter, the Civil Rights Act of 1871, now codified as Section 1983, was created to give citizens the right to seek redress and to provide a federal court remedy against all forms of official violation of federally protected rights. Before *Monell*, however, while individual officials could be sued, municipalities could not. In this decision, the Court held that the Civil Rights Act of 1871 did apply to local governments; they were to be considered persons within the meaning of the Constitution. This decision opened the door for claims against municipalities.

To prevail, the plaintiff must show that the action taken by the municipality and claimed as unconstitutional implements or executes a policy, statement, ordinance, regulation, or decision officially adopted or put forth by those whose edicts or acts may fairly be said to represent official policy. In relation to law enforcement, the plaintiff has to prove that the action taken by an agency or its officers was the result of an official directive that turns out to be unconstitutional. The directive can be put forth by the agency or by someone who can be recognized as representing official agency policy.

The Court then took it a step further. It stated that a municipality may be sued for constitutional deprivations caused by a customary action, even if that action has not received formal approval through official decision-making channels. This creates tremendous potential for liability. In effect, it states that a municipality has law enforcement policies whether it chooses to develop them or not. If an agency does not outline a formal policy, the policy will be defined as the customary way specific situations are handled. Without a documented policy, this means that policy is created on the street, with the past history of actions by officers in making arrests and enforcing laws being opened to scrutiny. Such a situation will likely form the basis of a substantial liability judgment.

The limit to the *Monell* decision is that a direct connection must exist between the municipal conduct and the constitutional deprivation. The *Monell* decision itself stated that, while a municipality can be held liable when the action of the municipality itself caused the harm, it cannot be held "liable under a theory of *respondeat superior* for the actions of its employees." *Respondeat superior* is a legal doctrine that makes the person or agency in charge responsible for those acting under him or her. The Court held that an agency is not accountable for the actions of its officers simply because they work for it. The plaintiff must show that an agency policy was the driving force behind an incident. However, if an employee has a history of acting inappropriately, and this has not been addressed by the employee's supervisor, it might be argued that the employee's actions amount to a custom or policy.

The Court has held that the causation requirement of Section 1983 is a matter of statutory interpretation rather than common tort law. Negligence deals with the conduct of the officers involved in an incident, rather than the policy itself. As such, negligence alone is not sufficient to make a case in federal court. If a policy is in place that can pass constitutional muster, a single incident where officers failed to carry out that policy correctly will not result in a violation of a person's civil rights. This applies even if the inappropriate action was determined to be gross negligence. There has to be a pattern of unconstitutional actions or abuse. If such a pattern exists, it may be treated by a federal court as a custom or policy. Liability could also be attached, based on a theory of reckless disregard or deliberate indifference to the rights of the people within the city's domain. (The concept of deliberate indifference is discussed in the case of *Canton v. Harris.*)

Of course, if no connection can be made between municipal conduct and constitutional deprivation, the agency may not be off the hook. It simply means the plaintiff will not win based on a theory of violation of federal civil rights. Other venues may exist. In most cases, negligent behavior by officers will result in the agency paying damages of some sort.

Canton v. Harris

The position that claims against municipalities are actionable was expanded by *Canton v. Harris*, 489 U.S. 378 (1989). In that case, Ms. Harris was arrested by police officers in Canton, Ohio. After her arrest, she fell down several times and was incoherent. The officers summoned no medical assistance for her. She was later found to be suffering from several emotional ailments that required hospitalization for one week, and subsequent out-patient treatment for an additional year. Ms. Harris sued the city of *Canton* under 42 U.S.C. 1983 claiming that her rights under the due process clause of the Fourteenth Amendment were violated when she did not receive necessary medical attention while in police custody. The Supreme Court ruled that, even if a policy is constitutional, an unconstitutional application of that policy could create liability under Section 1983, if the improper action was due to a lack of adequate training.

The court knew it was expanding the *Monell* decision, stating that "*Monell*'s rule that a city is not liable under Section 1983 unless a municipal policy causes a constitutional deprivation will not be satisfied by merely alleging that the existing training program for a class of employees, such as police officers, represents the policy for which the city is responsible." In other words, an agency must do more than just have a training program in place.

The real issue "is whether that training program is adequate; and if it is not, the question becomes whether such inadequate training can justifiably be said to represent 'city policy.' It may seem contrary to common sense to assert that a municipality will actually have a policy of not taking reasonable steps to train its employees. But it may happen that in light of the duties assigned to specific officers or employees, the need for more or different training is so obvious, and the inadequacy so likely to result in the violation of constitutional rights, that the policy makers of the city can reasonably be said to have been deliberately indifferent to the need. In that event, the failure to provide proper training may fairly be said to represent a policy for which the city is responsible, and for which the city may be held liable if it actually causes injury."

While the facts of *Canton* involved the administration of first aid, the example used to explain the decision dealt with the use of force. The court noted that a city arms its officers with firearms in part to allow them to arrest fleeing felons. Therefore, "the need to train officers in the constitutional limitations on the use of deadly force can be said to be 'so obvious' that failure to do so could properly be characterized as 'deliberate indifference' to constitutional rights."

This need for more or different training is also obvious when the inadequacies routinely displayed by officers on the street are likely to result in the violation of constitutional rights. Thus, municipalities can be liable if their officers continuously perform specifically assigned tasks in an inappropriate manner, or consistently demonstrate bad judgment. (Appendix B provides a case study that illustrates this issue.)

The opening through which a claimant must pass to prove a "failure to train" theory is small. The Supreme Court made sure of this by the scope it applied to "deliberate indifference." To prove failure to train, the plaintiff must prove that the deficiency in training actually caused the officers to be indifferent to a person's constitutional rights. Furthermore, the identified deficiency in training must be closely related to the ultimate injury.

In *Farmer v. Brennan*, 511 U.S. 825 (1994), the Supreme Court provided a clear definition of deliberate indifference. In that case, the Court stated that deliberate indifference is equivalent to reckless disregard. It describes a state of mind where a condition of blame exists that is more than negligence, but something less than acts or omissions for the purpose of causing harm or with knowledge that harm will result. In other words, deliberate indifference involves more than a simple failure to act; it involves a conscious choice to not act when you know that this failure will probably result in serious consequences.

Deliberate indifference can also apply to the area of supervision. It is not enough that you provide training for specific tasks and the use of discretion. Once officers have been trained, they must be adequately supervised to ensure that the training they were given was appropriate, and that the officers perform their duties consistently with that training.

Tennessee v. Garner

While the Supreme Court is loathe to reverse itself, it has shown a willingness to take a fresh look at precedents established by other means. Based on changing social and technological standards, the court may adopt a new perspective in matters of policy and may apply that perspective to a review of how municipal governments treat individuals who interact with them. As a result, long-standing practices, customs, and even state laws that were once considered acceptable may now be ruled unconstitutional. This is what happened in *Tennessee v. Garner*, 471 U.S. 1 (1985).

In this case, a young man was killed while fleeing the scene of an apparent burglary. Although he was actively avoiding arrest, he was unarmed, and posed no threat. The city of Memphis allowed the use of deadly force in cases of burglary. In addition, the State of Tennessee had a statute stating that an officer, after giving notice of an intent to arrest a suspect, could use all necessary means to make the arrest if that person either flees or forcibly resists. This statute had been construed to mean that a person fleeing the scene of a burglary could be shot if that person did not stop for the police.

The Supreme Court did not find the Tennessee statute unconstitutional on its face. However, it did rule that whenever an officer restrains the freedom of a person to walk away, he or she has applied a seizure, which is subject to the reasonableness requirement of the Fourth Amendment. The court further ruled that the Tennessee statute allowing for the use of all necessary means to make an arrest did not give an officer the right to shoot and kill a suspect. As such, the statute was unconstitutional insofar as it authorized the use of deadly force against a fleeing person who was not dangerous.

The Supreme Court noted that the prevailing rule in common law had been that the use of deadly force against a fleeing felon was considered reasonable. The court further pointed out that the common law arose at a time when virtually all felonies were punishable by death. By the time of the Garner decision, however, almost all crimes formerly punished by death were no longer punished that way. In its decision, the court repeatedly made reference to studies involving deadly force and the FBI's classification of crime. For example, burglary is a property crime, not a violent one.

Furthermore, the court specifically noted the common law rule was developed when weapons were rudimentary and not very accurate. Over time, technological advances in firearms have made them extremely deadly. The increased efficiency of weapons caused the court to reconsider the policies under which they could be used.

Thus, the court has shown a willingness to review law enforcement policies and state statutes in light of a number of factors. These include updated methods of crime prevention, advances in technology and prevailing social standards regarding life, and the use of government sanctioned force to terminate it. As times change, the manner by which law enforcement agencies operate must change, as well. This is why policy development must be an ongoing process.

Discussion Questions

1. What was the decision in *Monell v. Dept. of Social Services of the City of New York*? What was its impact?

2. How is it possible for a law enforcement agency to have policies whether it has developed them or not?

3. What are the limiting aspects of the *Monell* decision?

4. What was the decision in *Canton v. Harris*? What was its affect?

5. What does deliberate indifference mean? How can it be established?

6. What was the decision in *Tennessee v. Garner*? How does that decision require law enforcement agencies to make policy development and review an ongoing process?

Three

Areas Policy Should Address

Objectives

In this chapter, you will learn the following:

- *Proactive reviews of current agency operations*
- *Specific areas where policies are needed*
- *Steps for identifying additional areas needing policies*

Not every aspect of law enforcement requires a policy. Too many policies can stifle an agency, breeding an over-reliance on stated procedures and rules. In addition, not all agencies need policies in the same areas. This chapter will help you identify the areas within your agency that policies should address.

Proactive Policy Management

Many law enforcement administrators focus their attention on problem areas. These administrators often seek refuge in policies after going through a serious incident, or when a neighboring jurisdiction is hit with a liability judgment. In cases where administrators exhibit a "reflex" response, they are often more concerned with getting a policy in place than with creating one that aligns with the department's basic goals and objectives. A policy developed reactively rarely solves the underlying problem.

On the other hand, you should never arbitrarily decide that a particular area constitutes a problem and put a policy in place just for the sake of doing it. A policy must be based on a certifiable need, and it must meet specific criteria and objectives, all of which must be well-established and documented. This requires proactive policy management.

Proactive policy management means identifying potential problem areas related to policy, and then dealing with them before they reach a crisis stage. Key components of proactive policy management include the following:

- Understanding agency goals and mission statements to ensure that policies align correctly

- Periodically analyzing the current operations and practices of the agency, as well as applicable case law

- Identifying the areas that need to be covered by policies, but that currently are not

- Identifying resources for updating and reviewing policies as needed

- Developing a process for creating, approving, and updating policies and procedures

Before you can proactively manage policy, you must first understand your agency's goals and mission. Only then can you accurately analyze existing operations.

Analyze Existing Operations and Practices

Using your agency's goals and mission as guideposts, review the current operations and practices within your agency. Understanding the current status of your agency will enable you to accurately identify the areas where changes need to be made. In effect, you need to step back from your role as an agency administrator and to objectively analyze what your officers are doing on the street. This task has the following goals:

- Identifying and, if necessary, documenting existing policies and procedures.

- Making sure those policies and procedures are in alignment with the local jurisdiction (both the community in general and the agency's empowering body).

- Determining whether the policies and procedures are being practiced and enforced.

- Examining discretionary practices to see if they are consistent with the department's goals and objectives.

If you have a large agency, you may want to enlist some assistance in gathering information and conducting the analysis. Be sure to schedule enough time for this activity. The results of your analysis will determine the direction of policy and procedure development until the next review period.

Resources for Conducting Agency Reviews

Regardless of agency size, you have the following resources available:

- Existing policies

- Incident reports

- Files of past litigation proceedings

- Your own observations

- Interviews with other administrators, supervisors, and line officers

- Input from technical and legal experts on specific areas in question

Your particular agency may have additional resources available. In your initial review, be sure to document which resources you used and were available so that you can be consistent in future reviews. As additional resources become available, you may want to add them to the list.

Use of Case Law in Policy Development

After analyzing current operations, follow the guidelines presented by the three cases discussed in the previous chapter.

Monell v. Dept. of Social Services of the City of New York established that a municipality is considered to be a person within the meaning of the Constitution and can be sued, based on 42 USC Section 1983:

- Concentrate your efforts on those areas where officers interact with members of the public.

- Analyze existing policies to ensure no directive calls for action that may be considered a constitutional violation.

- Review areas where a potential exists for civil rights violations to occur.

Canton v. Harris established that municipal liability can be attached when a failure to train amounts to deliberate indifference to the rights of people with whom law enforcement officers come into contact:

- Review duties officers are expected to carry out, especially those that are likely to result in the violation of person's constitutional rights if they are not performed properly.

- Determine whether it is obvious that such a violation will likely occur unless officers receive more (or different) training.

Tennessee v. Garner determined that matters of policy are subject to review at any time.

- Establish periodic reviews of existing procedures to evaluate how they affect the populous they are designed to protect. Procedures that are constitutional now may be unconstitutional later.

- Evaluate how changing social standards, new equipment, and new technologies affect the operational aspects of existing standards and procedures.

- Review and amend existing procedures to reflect the impact of any new piece of equipment.

Areas to Address in Policy

All law enforcement agencies need to address certain areas. To identify those areas, remember the *Canton v. Harris* case. If it is obvious that officers need to be trained in a particular duty, it is also obvious that you need a policy to define and to clarify that duty. Clearly define both the operational procedures associated with the duty and the parameters for officer discretion. Of course, the question then becomes "what are those duties?"

First Aid

The facts in *Canton v. Harris* revolved around making a decision about whether a person in custody needed medical care. The court felt that law enforcement personnel will obviously encounter people in need of first aid, which creates a duty in that area. Since officers require training in first aid, every agency should have a first-aid policy. In addition, the passage of the Health Insurance Portability and Accountability Act (HIPAA) requires that law enforcement work with the medical community to develop policies that comply with the act and still enable law enforcement to collect the evidence that they need (see Appendix C for more information about HIPAA).

Use of Force

As the court stated in the *Canton v. Harris* decision, if an agency supplies its officers with firearms, it is obvious that they must be trained on the "the constitutional limitations on the use of deadly force." Deadly force can involve more than just the use of firearms, however, and includes any method of apprehending or restraining a suspect that might result in serious injury or death. Policy makers must address this issue, and must create training programs on any substances or weapons that are sanctioned for use-of-force situations.

New Technology

As new methods become available for apprehending and restraining suspects, policy makers need to review current policies, and possibly develop new ones to incorporate the new technology in daily operations. For instance, the use of pepper spray is an application of force that can have serious, if not deadly, consequences on some members of the population. Its growing usage almost guarantees that an officer will eventually come in contact with a person who will suffer an extreme reaction. Tasers are another example where a non-lethal use of force can have serious consequences if the person falls and hurts themselves. See "Incorporating New Technologies into Policies" on page 98.

Emergency Vehicle Operations

Law enforcement officers come into contact with citizens during pursuits and emergency responses. The need for training with respect to operating motor vehicles under these circumstances is likewise obvious. It, too, should be addressed by policy.

Domestic Violence and Stalking

Most jurisdictions mandate certain responses by law enforcement during domestic violence calls. As such, the need to train officers has become so obvious that failure to do so might be characterized as "deliberate indifference" to constitutional rights. Again, a need to train implies a need for policy.

Stalking is often related to domestic violence, but there are difficulties inherent in protecting the victim of stalking. In these cases, the perpetrator engages in a campaign of intimidation that seeks to evade the legal requirements for a successful prosecution. Meanwhile, the victim's life is completely disrupted by the need for constant vigilance. Many states have devised statutes that make stalking a crime, but enforcing these statutes can be challenging. Training officers to effectively handle such cases is imperative.

Sex Crimes

While most jurisdictions have statutes dictating law enforcement's response to these crimes, in some communities, law enforcement officers still have difficulty working appropriately with victims of these crimes. Because of the nature of these crimes, it is vital that officers understand how to treat the victims sensitively and appropriately. The consequences of not doing so further traumatize the victim, may prevent law enforcement from apprehending the perpetrator, or may damage the prosecution's chances for convicting the perpetrator, if the victim is unable to testify.

Conversely, there is a rising trend of false reporting. By developing consistent policies for working with both the victims and the suspects, law enforcement can help ensure that justice is truly served.

Missing Persons

Several high-profile cases and the passage of the Amber Alert legislation have changed the way law enforcement agencies handle missing-person cases, and how they work with other agencies on these cases. As such, policy makers need to review their existing policies to ensure that they align with current legislation and with the policies of surrounding jurisdictions.

Identifying Other Policy Needs

Individual agencies will likely have additional areas where policies are required. Again, do not arbitrarily identify an issue, and then implement some policy just for the sake of doing it. Use a proactive review process to determine specific needs, and use the following factors as indicators that a policy may be needed:

- **Court decisions:** Analyze court cases to determine if a new standard is being created that might require new training and policy. Once a policy has been developed, review it after each new relevant court decision to see if the policy continues to fit within the scope of reasonableness.

- **Citizen complaints:** If the same sort of problems occur repeatedly, clarify or redefine the agency's position on each of them. Depending on the gravity of the incidents, you may need to develop additional policies to address them.

- **Mandates or recommendations:** Newly passed legislation may assign additional responsibilities that are best addressed by policy. Also, recommendations from legal and risk management departments may point to emerging areas of concern.

- **Emerging, nationally accepted standards:** Keep track of professional boards and associations to discover what procedures they are addressing. These practices tend to be incorporated by many agencies and applied to court cases through the testimony of expert witnesses. As their use becomes widespread, they begin to take the form of standards.

If an area needs to be addressed, you must decide how and when to do it. If the issue revolves around an existing policy, amending the policy may not really be necessary. Instead, the problem relates to the officers' ability to carry out its directives. In this case, you may be able to resolve the situation by providing additional training, either immediately or during normal in-service schedules.

Often, the solution requires only a minor adjustment to a procedure or task. One agency reviewed its vehicle operations policy and decided to provide more training because its insurance carrier was concerned about an increase in vehicular accidents. It turned out that all the officers were coming in at noon to get their paychecks, which clogged the parking lot and led to more backing collisions. After evaluating why the accidents were happening, the agency solved the problem by simply posting a directive that officers could pick up their paychecks only at the end of their individual shifts.

Sometimes, however, you may discover that an existing policy must be overhauled, or that a completely new policy is required. For this reason, it is important to identify resources for reviewing and recommending policy changes, and to institute a systematic policy development process. The next chapters explain these aspects of policy development.

Regardless, you need to base your policy decisions on true needs that you have identified, not on some self-imposed limitations from the past. The limitations cited most often include the size of the agency, its financial position, its geographic location, its available equipment, and the technical expertise of its personnel. These limitations can be valid restrictions, but they may not hold up over time. During the policy review, you must ask, "Has anything changed since the last time these issues were considered that would refute any or all of the restrictions?" Your answer should not be the result of speculation. Any decision you make must be documented and supported by strong empirical data that can withstand scrutiny.

Discussion Questions

1. What is meant by proactive policy development?

2. What steps should be taken to ascertain current agency operations and practices?

3. What are the guidelines set by case law for a proactive policy review?

4. What are the specific areas of law enforcement that require policies?

5. What are the guidelines for determining what additional areas should be addressed by policy?

Four

Planning the Development Process

Objectives

In this chapter, you will learn the following:

- *Importance of consistent process in policy development*
- *List of preliminary needs*
- *Available personnel for policy development*
- *Policy development plan*

It is not enough that you have a policy in place. The policy must accomplish the following tasks:

- Provide guidance for the officers.
- Reduce liability exposure for the agency.
- Enable you to defend the policy if it is ever challenged.

Having a process that meets all these objectives requires planning.

Understanding the Importance of Consistency

While a consistent process for creating and maintaining policies might not prevent someone from suing the agency, it will enable you to defend the policy and the decisions that lie behind the policy in question. A consistent process also enables you to accomplish the following goals:

- Prevents you from having to reinvent the wheel every time you need a new policy or procedure.
- Ensures no steps are left out of the process.

- Provides a level of comfort and transparency to the community by showing policies are created purposefully and thoughtfully.

- Enables you to respond to a crisis situation more quickly.

- Provides a level of comfort and familiarity to the officers and other team members who follow the policy because the same decision-making process is used every time.

- Prevents the appearance of any conflicts of interest because policy development is handled the same way each time.

- Gives the agency more credibility in court if the procedure is repeatable and the agency can demonstrate consistency.

- Improves the chances of the process being properly documented for historical purposes.

- Makes it easier to hand off responsibility to a new person or committee when necessary.

Getting Started

Every process has a starting point. When it comes to policy development, first use your review of agency operations and other factors to compile a list of issues you want the policy to address. Without well-defined targets, you will likely miss the mark, and the resulting policy won't achieve its objectives.

This list does not need be a formal document. It does not have to be complete, nor does it have to agree with what is addressed in the final policy. Its sole purpose is to assist you in planning and prioritizing the policy development process. While you can use any format for the list that serves your purpose, you might need to show your decision-making process, so save the list.

In addition, save any documents or information that you used to build the preliminary list of issues. This means retaining copies of reports, complaints, memos, laws, briefs, and so on. With this information on file, you can refer to it throughout the development process and can produce it as evidence to support your defense, if necessary.

Once the list is compiled, identify the personnel you need to participate in the process. Policy should not be written by one person in a back room. Instead, use a group of people from a variety of backgrounds to ensure that the final policy meets the needs of both the community and the agency. You will want to use both personnel from within the agency and members of the larger community. In fact, you may want to establish a standing committee where members rotate on and off after a specified term. Doing so will give you continuity and consistency in the decision-making process.

When it comes to agency personnel, there is no requirement that a particular number of people participate. However, committees are most effective when limited to 6-9 primary participants who then collect and coordinate additional feedback from their functional areas. The key is that every level or section that will be affected by a policy should have input into the policy's formulation.

Primary Agency Resources and Positions

Use agency personnel to fill the following critical roles.

- **Risk manager or other central figure in charge—** This is crucial; one person must manage the process to ensure the whole process goes forward and is completed. As the person responsible for mitigating the risk of incidents and lawsuits, the risk manager is the logical person to drive the policy development and review process. (In smaller agencies, the chief and risk manager are often one and the same person.) If the chief or risk manager delegates this role, that person must have the authority to keep the process on track. Too often, policy discussions never leave the talking stage because no one has the authority to drive them forward.

- **Line officers**—Too often line officers, who must follow the policy once it's implemented, are not consulted on policy matters. Instead, they are handed a policy from on high and told to follow it, even if it does not reflect street reality. In that situation, it is no wonder line officers often view policies as merely attempts to protect management from liability exposure. On the other hand, having line officers participate in the process gives them a sense of ownership in the policy. When they see a policy is geared toward their safety, they will be more likely to observe it.

- **Supervisors**—Like line officers, supervisors represent current field practices. Their involvement is crucial because they have to enforce the policy with the line officers. If they play a key role in developing and writing the policy, they will be compelled to enforce it.

- **Coordinator to maintain a document repository**— One person must be responsible for organizing data and making it available for consideration. This information includes copies of reports, complaints, community input, legal statutes, and the research that will be conducted. Maintaining a centralized document repository provides the foundation for documenting the group's activities. Centralizing and coordinating the documentation also ensures that at least one complete source contains the historical record for a policy. This position can be filled by a person appointed to the resource group specifically for this purpose, or can be assigned to someone already in the group.

- **Policy writer**—While the group determines which policies need to be addressed and identifies the priorities, the policy writer develops the documents based on the group's input, and incorporates review comments. Having a trained writer in this position can greatly facilitate the policy development process by ensuring that policies are clearly written and consistent in appearance.

Secondary Resources

You can also use a number of people from outside the agency. While the list below is not all-inclusive, it will give you an idea of the types of people you may want to include. You may need other people to participate as well, depending upon the importance of the policy and the degree of outside interest in that particular area of law enforcement/public safety.

- **Agency support and advisory groups**—These groups might include risk managers, attorneys, and anyone else who serves in an advisory capacity to the agency. They can provide the perspective of those whose primary purpose is to minimize the liability exposure of the agency.

- **Representatives from governing bodies**—These people can be observers or participants. In either case, including these representatives will educate them about the complex tasks of law enforcement. Doing so may prevent legislators from attempting to fill perceived policy voids by passing laws that have unintended consequences. On the other hand, if you proactively address policy issues and include lawmakers in the process, you might positively influence the laws affecting your operations.

- **Community at-large**—A law enforcement agency is ultimately responsible to the community it serves. Bringing in members of the community helps you identify their particular expectations and concerns. Community members can also provide the civilian perspective that sometimes goes unnoticed and may enable you to prevent potentially serious problems with a policy. Since the public comprises the juries that decide cases, having them involved before a policy is implemented is better than having an incident result in a court proceeding.

Team Organization

You can use an organizational chart to identify the names and functions of each committee member (Figure 1). In addition, it is a good idea to briefly list the duties and expectations for each committee member so that everyone understands not only his/her own role, but the role of the other members as well.

Resource Group

Risk Manager/ Group Leader

| Community Representatives | Administrator | Policy Writer | Document Coordinator | Supervisor |

Line Officers

Figure 1: Organizational Chart of Resource Group Members

Putting a Plan Together

To have a good, workable policy, you need to plan, especially if you are confronted with a critical issue. Taking the time to plan in the beginning will save double that time later by giving everyone a road map for development and ensuring that everyone understands the schedule and priorities. Planning involves the following steps:

1. Establish a schedule for the entire policy process.

   a. Set a date by which you want the policy to be implemented, then work backward to establish the milestones for each step. It's important to leave a reasonable amount of time for each activity.

   b. Include time for training in the schedule. A policy is not fully implemented until everyone has been trained.

   c. Update the schedule as you work through the process. It's more important that the policy is done correctly than that the exact dates are met; if you need more time for an activity, take it, but document that decision.

2. Assign someone to document the priorities and decisions made by the committee (for example, which policies are being developed first and why, meeting minutes, and so on). It's easier and more effective to have one person responsible for documenting decisions and action items. These documents help to ensure that the team continues to move forward instead of constantly revisiting the same issues. In addition, action items ensure accountability with the team.

3. Set up and maintain a project log. This can be a valuable management tool and can serve as an overview of the project (Figure 2).

   a. Allot spaces for start and completion of each activity.

   b. Track action items, including who's responsible for them and the due dates.

4. Decide on and set up a consistent format and layout for the policies and procedures. (See Chapter 6, "Writing Policy", for a more detailed discussion.)

Project Log

Policy_____ Person in Charge:_____

Event	Date Begun		Date Completed	
	Scheduled	Actual	Scheduled	Actual
1. List of preliminary issues				
2. Appointment of resource group				
3. Initial meeting of resource group				
4. Research of assigned topics				
5. Establish policy components (including tasks and procedures)				
6. First draft of policy				
7. First draft reviewed and discussed by resource group				
8. Second draft of policy				
9. Outside reviews				
10. Discussion of outside reviews				
11. Final draft of policy				
12. Final draft approved				
13. Policy training				
14. Policy put into effect				

Figure 2: Project Log

Developing a Policy

The following list describes the activities that occur during the policy development process.

1. **Convene the resource group.** After selecting the committee members, bring them together to begin work. During the first meeting, a key objective is to expand your preliminary list of issues. This discussion ensures that the group agrees on what should be addressed and on what the priorities are.

2. **Assign action items and due dates.** When working with a group of people, it is important to document who is assigned to each action item and to identify a deadline for completing the item. This provides accountability and ensures progress toward the goal.

3. **Conduct research.** The revised preliminary list of issues serves as the basis of research conducted by the group. This research will confirm whether an issue or problem should be addressed through policy, or whether it can be better handled by some other means. This research may also identify additional policy issues. The group should use sources, such as current field practices, court decisions, and community expectations.

4. **Establish tasks and procedures.** After identifying the issues, the group determines the tasks for handling those issues. For each task, the group identifies a set of procedures explaining how officers must perform that task.

5. **Write a draft of the policy.** Using a standardized format, write a draft of the policy, keeping in mind that the primary audience is line officers. To that end, the writing style should be concise and easy to understand. Using a trained technical writer can be invaluable, particularly if you have a lot of policies and procedures to document.

6. **Have the draft reviewed.** After writing the draft, disseminate it for review among the functional groups affected by the policy. This feedback serves as another round of research. This time, your objective is to discover what people think about the planned policy. After the group evaluates the comments, the writer incorporates the comments into a final draft, ensuring that the group has acted on the applicable recommendations. If some recommendations are not implemented, the group needs to document the reason

for not implementing them and communicate the reason back to the reviewers.

7. **Implement the policy.** Once the policy is issued, train the officers to it. Training consists of providing the officers with the policy, giving them an opportunity to ask questions about it, and having them acknowledge in writing that they understand, and will abide by, the purpose of the policy and its prescribed directives.

8. **Set enforcement expectations.** Supervisors are primarily responsible for enforcing policies. For this reason, you should strive at all times to reinforce their sense of ownership in the policy. This includes establishing programs of reporting and debriefings that will facilitate both enforcement and policy maintenance.

9. **Conduct ongoing analysis.** Create a system to provide ongoing feedback on the policy, so that it can be reinforced or altered as needed. The policy itself should explain how feedback should be handled and should provide for a periodic review of procedures.

The remaining chapters in this book describe the above steps in more detail.

Discussion Questions

1. What is the starting point for developing a policy?

2. Why should policy be developed by a group instead of by one person?

3. What agency resources and positions should be represented on a policy group? What are the roles of each?

4. What outside resources should be represented on a policy group? What are the roles of each?

5. What factors will help determine the size of the policy group?

Five

Developing Policy

Objectives

In this chapter, you will learn how to do the following:

- *Set an agenda for the initial meeting*
- *Conduct research on policy issues*
- *Make decisions based on research*
- *Identify required components for all policies*
- *Identify additional components for a policy*

Once a plan is in place, the real work of developing the policy begins. As mentioned in the previous chapter, this process needs to be a group effort to ensure that the policy accounts for the concerns of each functional area. Line officers and supervisors have a perspective based on current field practices, while risk managers and attorneys focus on issues of liability. Members of the general public can give a sense of the community's expectations, as well as providing those of individual citizens.

Setting an Agenda for the Initial Meeting

The initial meeting has the following objectives:

- Ensure that all members have a clear understanding of the process by going over the plan in depth.

- Provide an opportunity for the group to voice any concerns about the plans and process. If problems exist, consider making alterations as necessary. You want everyone to do more than just understand the plan; you want them to agree with it, as well.

- Discuss the issues that you want the policy to address. Present your list of preliminary needs and allow the individual members to add their own ideas. This will enable you to compile a set of concerns from many different viewpoints.

- Divvy up research and other responsibilities, and determine the due dates.

- Review schedules and set future meetings, action items, and milestones.

The following agenda (Figure 3) provides an example of how you might structure the initial meeting.

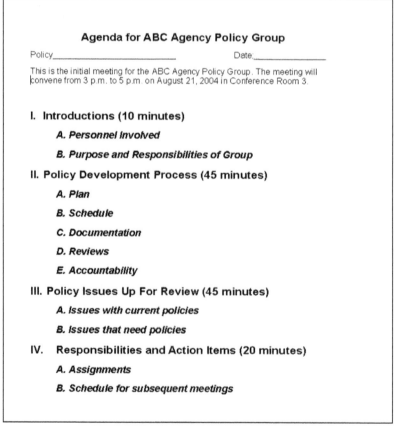

Agenda for ABC Agency Policy Group

Policy_____   Date:_____

This is the initial meeting for the ABC Agency Policy Group. The meeting will convene from 3 p.m. to 5 p.m. on August 21, 2004 in Conference Room 3.

I. Introductions (10 minutes)

    A. Personnel Involved

    B. Purpose and Responsibilities of Group

II. Policy Development Process (45 minutes)

    A. Plan

    B. Schedule

    C. Documentation

    D. Reviews

    E. Accountability

III. Policy Issues Up For Review (45 minutes)

    A. Issues with current policies

    B. Issues that need policies

IV.   Responsibilities and Action Items (20 minutes)

    A. Assignments

    B. Schedule for subsequent meetings

Figure 3: Sample Agenda

In many respects, this early discussion is really a brainstorming exercise so the group can compile all possible issues for consideration. At this point, the group needs to consider any issue raised as a valid concern and incorporate it into the research activities. Once the research is completed, the group will determine whether or not such issues will be addressed in the final policy.

Be flexible about the amount of time allotted for research. You do not want to rush the process to the point where the data is incomplete or faulty. If someone needs additional time to finish valid research, or to follow a lead in a new direction, that person should have the leeway to do so. On the other hand, without a deadline of some sort, many people tend to put off completing action items. All members should leave the initial meeting with a clear idea about what their next step is and how long they have before they are required to report back.

Conducting Research on Policy Issues

During the research phase, you need to find out how the assigned set of issues apply to current practices, policies, and expectations.

Identifying Research Sources

The following sections describe the sources for collecting this information.

- **Risk managers and legal affairs officers**—Proactive policy development requires a strategic perspective and a broad view. Risk managers and legal advisors frequently work with many other agencies, so they not only see the implications of issues, but also see best practices. Such best practices can then be discussed with the policy group.

- **Line officers**—The best way to find out about street reality is to ride with the line officers. Civilian policy group members may find this particularly useful, as long as such a practice is allowed by the agency. (Of course, before participating in such an event, civilians must be apprised of the risks involved and sign any required waivers of responsibility.)

It is important that line officers understand that the purpose for the research is to help them do their jobs safely and effectively, and is not being used for possible disciplinary action. If the officers know their input will be considered, they will likely be forthcoming with information.

- **Incident reports**—You can also discern a great deal about street reality by reviewing incident reports. Such reports describe the day-to-day experiences of line officers as they interact with the public, and can identify potential issues where policy is needed. Adding questions to the report form may assist you in identifying specific issues.

- **Supervisors**—Supervisors can also provide accurate reports of what happens on the street. Because they oversee operational practices, they may be able to give you a broader view of an issue than line officers. As with line officers, ensure that you emphasize that such research is intended to assist the supervisors in doing their jobs safely and effectively.

- **Supervisor reports**—These reports may provide additional insight into street reality. Adding some specific questions to these report forms may assist you in information gathering about specific issues.

- **Complaints**—Complaint reports can be used in both the planning and research stages. During the planning phase, similar types of complaints can indicate a need to address an issue. During the research phase, review the complaints more thoroughly to understand what happened in each incident, and to determine whether or not a pattern exists among them. Also, complaints filed by citizens against an agency give you an idea of the tolerance level within the community. This level of tolerance will affect how you refine existing procedures and develop new ones.

- **General public**—While including community members in the policy group gives you some information about the community, you can use public forums to give other community members an opportunity to be heard. A forum presents a more accurate picture of the public's expectations of the agency, and can be another source for understanding the public's tolerance for current and proposed procedures. Public forums might not be needed for all policy areas, but consider using them for high-profile policies, or for policies that deal with larger liability issues.

- **Court decisions**—Review and evaluate all precedent-setting decisions for their impact on the proposed policy. These decisions establish the standards that your agency must abide by and will be judged against in the future.

- **Policies of other agencies**—Reviewing a sample of policies from other agencies and organizations can be very useful. These policies may address areas that the policy group did not think of, and may show possible ways to handle sensitive issues. It is best to use policies that come from departments similar to yours in terms of size, community served, and resources available.

However, *use these policies as reference material only*; you cannot simply adopt another agency's policy as your own. (By the same token, when it comes to documentation, you cannot simply adopt the forms used by another agency or the samples provided in this book. Design your forms to reflect the specific needs of your agency.) See Appendix A, "Sample Policy".

Documenting the Research and Making Decisions

As always, keep accurate records of your research. For reports, complaints, court decisions, or policies from other agencies, keep a copy of each piece of information. To document interviews with officers and members of the general public, compile a detailed set of notes that identify the name and position of the person interviewed, the date and time of the interview, and a summary of the person's responses, as well as any supporting information that the person provides you. If questioned later, you cannot simply say "I talked to this person who said that...." You have to be able to produce all supporting material that contributed to a decision. (See Chapter 6, "Writing Policy", for more information.)

Once the group completes the research, members can reconvene to decide which items on the preliminary list still apply and to identify the priorities for addressing them. If research does not substantiate an issue, don't address it in a policy. To do so would only add unnecessary material.

If you do eliminate an item from the list, document why you made that decision. This documentation comprises a crucial part of the record if you are ever challenged. If somebody later says you knew about a problem but did nothing about it, you can counter by saying something to the effect of "Yes, we did know about that, and it was considered. However, it was not addressed by policy because...." Again, it is not crucial that everyone agrees with your policy; you just have to prove it was developed in a reasonable manner.

In addition, just because an item is not a problem now does not mean it will not be one later. Including all the data in the file provides a valuable resource if you decide to revisit an issue later. Thus, documenting your decisions when paring down the initial list enables you to win in two ways:

- Provides a defense for today's action

- Gives you a starting point for tomorrow's research and analysis

Developing Components of a Policy

Eliminating the unnecessary items establishes which issues must be addressed by the policy. After identifying those areas, the policy group can begin to develop the individual components of a policy. While some policies require more components than others, all policies should include the following components. (See Appendix A, "Sample Policy", for a model policy.)

Basic Components of Policy

The following sections describe the basic components of a policy and show examples from several policies provided by the Michigan Municipal League (MML). To see a complete model policy, see Appendix A, "Sample Policy."

- **Policy statement and rationale**—This statement explains why policy is needed in a particular area. For example, MML's *Use of Force* policy states:

  This Department will employ the amount of force that is reasonable and necessary to overcome the resistance offered, effect a lawful arrest, and/or accomplish the lawful performance of duty while protecting the public.

- **Statutory reference**—If the policy is governed by statute, include that statute in the policy, either by quoting the law directly or by restating it in a manner that is easy to understand. For example, if you modify your missing child policy, you would want to reference the Amber Alert legislation. As another example, the MML's *Police Operation of Motor Vehicles* policy states the following:

  A. Michigan Vehicle Code MCLA 257.603 - provides in pertinent part:

  "The provisions of this chapter... apply to the drivers of all vehicles owned or operated by [any political subdivision] of the state, subject to the specific exceptions as are set forth... with reference to authorized emergency vehicles."

"The driver of an authorized emergency vehicle when responding to an emergency call... may exercise the privileges set forth in this section, subject to the conditions of this section."

"The driver of an authorized emergency vehicle may:

* Park or stand irrespective of the provisions of this act.

* Proceed through a red or stop signal or stop sign but only after slowing down as may be necessary to allow for safe operation.

* Exceed the prima facie speed limit so long as he does not endanger life or property.

* Disregard regulations governing direction or movement or turning in specified direction."

B. Michigan Vehicle Code MCLA 257.632 - provides in pertinent part:

"The speed limitations set forth in this chapter shall not apply to vehicles when operated with due regard for safety under the direction of the police when traveling in emergencies or in the chase or apprehension of violators of the law or of persons charged with or suspected of a violation. *This exemption shall not, however, protect the driver of the vehicle from the consequences of a reckless disregard of the safety of others.*" (Emphasis added)

C. Even though legally engaged in emergency driving or pursuit, an officer is not relieved of the duty to drive with "due regard" for the safety of all persons, nor is an officer protected from the consequences of any reckless disregard for the safety of others.

- **Definitions**—Some terms can vary from agency to agency, so define the exact meaning of legal terminology. To reduce ambiguity, also clearly define any term that may cause confusion among your officers. This section is typically completed after the first draft. To determine what terms to include, review the draft and list all terms that need further clarification. For example, MML's *Use of Force* policy defines the following terms:

- Control
- Lethal Force
- Force
- Last Resort
- Less Lethal Force
- Reasonableness
- Resistance

- **Procedures**—Policies are primarily intended to guide line officers, so focus the procedures on the actions that officers need to take. To confine an officer to a set of specific procedures, carefully define the exact steps you want the officer to take. On the other hand, to provide officers with discretion in a particular area, define the parameters of that discretion, as well as the escalation path if the circumstances exceed the discretionary powers given the officers.

The number of procedures and steps depend on the area being addressed. However, the most effective procedures contain 10 or fewer steps, so you may want to separate an incident into various stages, including a procedure for each stage. For instance, a policy on emergency vehicle operations may address an officer's role and responsibility in the areas of initiating, continuing, and terminating a pursuit.

Procedures also need to address the role of other officers who may become involved in an incident as assisting officers. These roles and responsibilities need to link with the procedures describing the primary officer's role. Doing so ensures that everyone understands their own responsibilities and those of the other members of their group, as well as how those responsibilities complement each other. MML's *Post-force Reporting Policy* shows several examples of procedures. (See Appendix A.)

- **Supervision**—The supervisory component provides operational guidelines for a supervisor during an incident and describes how a policy will be enforced. For example, MML's *Police Operation of Motor Vehicles* policy indicates several guidelines for supervisors during a pursuit, including:

  - Supervisors direct the number of units involved
  - Supervisors can teminate the pursuit at any time
  - Officers must receive permission from the supervisor before intentionally colliding with a suspect's vehicle during a pursuit.

- **Interjurisdictional matters**—If officers might interact with other agencies when following a policy, the policy should provide guidelines for the interaction. With passage of the Homeland Security Act, it is even more critical that everyone involved understands their roles and the rules for interaction. For this reason, it is important for neighboring jurisdictions to work together and to understand each other's policies on interjurisdictional situations.

  For example, a policy on pursuits needs to include guidelines for what to do when a pursuit crosses jurisdictional boundaries. MML's *Police Operation of Motor Vehicles* policy provides the following:

  A. When a pursuit initiated by an outside police agency enters our jurisdiction, the initiating unit and jurisdiction remains responsible for the progress and conduct of the pursuit.

  B. This agency's personnel and vehicles shall not become involved in any such pursuit unless they are directed to do so by proper authority, in accordance with this policy.

  C. This order shall govern the conduct and actions of this agency's personnel once they are committed.

- **Apprehension**—If officers might arrest a suspect while following a policy, the policy should include procedures for taking suspects into custody. However, since apprehension is a seizure and can be construed as a use of force, some agencies opt to develop a separate, stand-alone policy for custody procedures. In this case, provide a cross-reference to the custody procedures in the policies that may result in apprehension of a suspect.

- **Post-incident responsibilities**—This section explains the procedures and deadlines for reporting an incident. Such reporting enables you to compile information about an incident and to evaluate an officer's conformity to the policy.

The section also should include a procedure for conducting post-incident reviews and debriefings, which should occur regardless of whether disciplinary action is needed. The review reinforces the policy and enables officers to know where they stand.

In addition, establish a system for officers and supervisors to provide feedback on the effectiveness of a policy. Such feedback enables you to proactively amend the policy if it becomes outdated or ineffective. For example, MML's *Use of Weapons and Restraints* policy indicates the following post-incident requirements:

> Whenever an officer uses an authorized weapon as a means of controlling resistive behavior, or uses any other object as a weapon pursuant to the "Last Resort" provisions of the Department's Use of Force policy, said use shall be reported as prescribed in the Post Force Reporting Process.

- **Training**—Before a policy can be fully implemented, officers must understand the policy's requirements and procedures. This section describes the process for certifying that officers have been trained to the policy, as well as the re-certification requirements. Providing explicit training requirements conveys the agency's commitment to the policy and to keep officers trained.

In addition, this section should explain how to properly document the training. For example, MML's *Use of Weapons and Restraints* policy states the following:

This department is committed to the mandatory training of all sworn officers in the use of department-authorized weapons.

A. Department subject-control training program on a periodic basis.

B. Department firearm training at least (four) times a year. The training applies to all firearms authorized or approved for law enforcement purposes, including the primary duty weapon, backup weapon, off-duty weapon, shotgun, carbine, rifle, or any other firearm.

C. Demonstrated proficiency with any authorized weapons, prior to their issue or carry. This shall apply to restraint devices, aerosol weapons, impact weapons, less lethal force weapons and any other weapons which an officer is equipped or is authorized to carry.

    1.Continued proficiency in subject-control techniques and the use of authorized weapons is recognized as a required job skill, necessary to continue employment as a police officer.

    2.Failure to successfully complete the required training at the assigned frequencies, or to demonstrate proficiency in the use of any authorized weapon, will result in one or both of the following administrative actions:

        a. the revocation of authorization to carry or use the weapon in question;

        b.discipline, up to and including discharge. At the department's discretion, the department may take reasonable steps to provide the officer with additional or remedial training.

- **Discipline**—For a policy to be effective, officers must understand the consequences of not abiding by the policy. This section describes the disciplinary proceedings, and provides supervisors with guidelines for disciplining those officers who deviate from the policy.

- **Other components**—A policy may include other components, depending upon the needs of the policy group. The group may want to increase the weight given to a particular issue by highlighting its coverage. For example, in an emergency vehicle operations policy, the section on terminating pursuits might include roadblocks. However, since a roadblock can be considered a use of force, the policy group may opt to address it as a stand-alone item, highlighting the specific restrictions.

Tracking Policy Development

Keeping track of a policy's development can be a daunting task. The following worksheet (Figure 4 and Figure 4a) can assist you in focusing the research, in evaluating status, and in identifying remaining action items.

Project Worksheet

Policy_____   Date:_____

Policy Statement and Rationale
- Why does the agency want to develop a policy in this area? What statements support this need?
- What are an officer's general duties relating to this area?

Statutory Reference
- Is the policy area governed by statute?
- Can the statute be quoted directly or should it be restated for ease of understanding?

Procedural Aspects
- Can an incident be separated into stages? If so, what are they and should each stage be addressed as an individual component?
- What general tasks will an officer be expected to perform when confronted with an incident or stage of an incident? For each task, what procedures should be followed in carrying it out?
- For those tasks left up to discretion, what parameters should an officer use when formulating a course of action?
- Are any tasks so critical that they should be addressed as stand-alone components?
- Will other officers typically interact with the primary officer during an incident? If so, should specific functions (such as backup, communications, etc.), be addressed as separate components? What are the responsibilities of each officer involved and what procedures should be used to carry out those responsibilities?
- If there is potential for injury to anyone involved in an incident, what medical assistance must an officer give?

Supervision
- What responsibilities will be assigned to a supervisor, both during and after an incident?

Discipline
- Relating to supervisory responsibilities, what disciplinary action should be taken if an officer does not conform to policy?
- If disciplinary measures are graduated, spell out what actions will be merited for both frequency of violation (i.e. first offense, second offense, etc.) and severity of violation.

Figure 4: Policy Development Status Worksheet (page 1)

Policy Worksheet (continued)

Interjurisdictional Matters

- What are the procedures for handling an incident that crosses jurisdictional lines or requires that officers interact with officers from other agencies?

Apprehension

- What procedures should be followed when taking a suspect into custody?

Post-Incident Responsibilities

- What after-action reports should be submitted? To whom should those reports be submitted and in what time frame?

- When should a review of an incident take place and what should be covered? Who should participate in such a review?

Training

- What is the process of certifying officers to policy?

- What is the process for recertification? How frequently should recertification be required?

Definitions

- What terms should to be clarified to show how the agency defines them?

- What legal terms need to be explained?

Figure 4a: Policy Development Status Worksheet (page 2)

Discussion Questions

1. What are the objectives for the initial meeting of the policy group?

2. What are the primary resources for researching a policy issue?

3. Why should an agency never simply adopt the policy of another agency?

4. Why should you document a decision to remove an issue from the preliminary list of needs?

5. What are the basic components of a policy?

6. Why should the procedural aspects of a policy focus on the responsibilities of line officers?

7. How can you determine which officers should be addressed in the procedural aspects of policy?

8. How can you increase the weight given to a particularly crucial issue?

Six

Writing Policy

Objectives

In this chapter, you will learn the following:

- *Write for the correct target audience*
- *Understand possible formats for policy*
- *Understand the initial review process for a policy draft*

Using the components identified by the policy group, as well as the policy templates, the policy writer develops the first draft.

Writing the first draft of the policy sounds like a simple task, but it's not. If the group does not clearly articulate its directives, the policy may be difficult to understand and interpret. Such difficulties could increase an agency's liability exposure and could negatively impact efficiency.

Putting a Draft Together

If you have a lot of policies and have the budget to do so, you may want to use an agency specialist to write and edit the policies for you. Bringing in a specialist at this point can also serve as a good check for the policy. For the writing process to work, you must clearly explain to the specialist what you want the policy to say. As the specialist is developing the draft using the information you provide, he or she may identify holes and inconsistencies that the group needs to address. In addition, if parts of the policy are unclear, the policy group may need to provide additional clarification. If you cannot accurately convey your directives to the specialist, you probably will not be able to convey them to your officers either.

If you decide to develop the draft yourself, remember the following keys to writing an effective first draft:

- Identify your audience.

- Use the principles of good writing.

- Ensure accuracy and completeness.

Identifying Your Audience

Too often policies are not geared to the proper audience. Policies written by administrators are usually written for administrators. This is not intentional; it just happens. Writing is not an easy task, so people tend to write in a manner with which they are most comfortable. In effect, they write for themselves rather than for their readers. They often make the mistake of believing that if something makes perfect sense to them, it will make perfect sense to everybody else, as well. Then, they blame the reader for not fully comprehending what is being said. It is important to realize, however, that in most miscommunication, the problem lies with the person sending the message, not the one receiving it.

Since the primary objective of any policy is to direct line officers and supervisors, they are the true audience. To keep the true audience in mind, picture the officers and supervisors in your mind as you write. Then, review the policy from the perspective of an officer or supervisor, and ensure that you get input from members of the audience.

Using the Principles of Good Writing

Write the policy in simple, clear language that officers can readily comprehend. At the same time, do not condescend or patronize the reader. The following tips will help you maintain this balance:

- **Use the KISS principle.** KISS stands for "Keep It Simple, Stupid." People frequently make ideas more difficult than they have to be. If a policy is not clear, officers will not be able to abide by it. Try to keep procedures to 10 or fewer steps. Use action verbs. Make each action a separate step. This will help officers remember the procedure more easily.

- **Avoid legal jargon and acronyms.** This relates to the KISS principle. Don't try to dazzle the courts and attorneys by using legal jargon and concepts. These are intimidating and can be difficult to grasp. If you do need to explain legal issues, use simple, everyday language. Line officers often interpret an abundance of legalese as an attempt by administrators to protect themselves from liability exposure. If you must use acronyms, be sure to define them.

- **Be concise.** The value of a policy is measured not by the number of pages but by its effectiveness. It should address what needs to be addressed, but no more. Superfluous information tends to clutter a document, making it more difficult to understand. Avoid long sentences; if the sentence is more than 25 words, break it up.

- **Make the policy a source of guidance.** Ideally, officers will look to a policy for direction and help. For that to happen, the policy needs to focus on the positive—the actions that the officers need to take in a particular situation. Avoid creating long lists of things not to do.

- **Use terminology consistently.** Follow the one word-one meaning rule. For example, if you use "agency" to mean the police department, then don't also use "agency" to mean an outside entity that the police department interacts with.

- **Use graphics where possible:** Officers and supervisors tend to be highly visual, so use graphics as appropriate to help clarify steps.

Ensuring Consistency and Completeness

Consider adopting a format you can use for all policies within the department. A standardized format makes policies easier to understand. If they all have the same feel, in both appearance and presentation, officers will know what to expect. Standardization helps officers focus on what is being said, not how it's being presented. A standard format also makes policy writing easier. The person writing a particular policy can take an established template and "fill in the blanks" as required.

The layout and organization of the policy needs to facilitate easy access to the information. Use what works best for your agency. One possibility is to use an "outline" format. To use an outline, identify the major sections using Roman numerals and bold-faced headings. Underneath the sections, use lettered sub-sections to identify additional details. In Figure 5, for example, it is very clear what a dispatcher and a supervisor will be responsible for in a pursuit.

VI. Responsibilities of Communications Personnel

A.   Upon notification that a pursuit is in progress, communications personnel shall immediately advise a supervisor of essential information regarding the pursuit.

B.   Communications personnel shall also carry out the following responsibilities during the pursuit:

1.   Receive and record all incoming information on the pursuit and the pursued vehicle

2.   Control all radio communications and clear the radio channels of all non-emergency calls

3.   Perform relevant record and motor vehicle checks

4.   Coordinate and dispatch back-up assistance and air support units under the direction of the field supervisor

5.   When practical, notify neighboring jurisdictions when a pursuit may extend into their location. With that notification, the communications personnel should specify whether involvement is requested, as determined by the supervisor's directives.

VII. Responsibilities of Supervisor

A.   After being notified of a department pursuit, a supervisor shall:

1.   Ensure proper radio channels and procedures are in use

2.   Ensure tactics conform with department policy

3.   Ensure only the necessary number of unit are involved

4.   Ensure allied agencies are notified

5.   Consider aborting the pursuit if cause exists

6.   Consider air support availability and practicality

Figure 5: Example of a Policy Format

Another possibility is to use an "all numbers" format to divide a policy into sections and subsections, as illustrated below. Whatever format you choose, be consistent. Write all policies the same way and use the same format for each one. (See Figure 6.)

---

6. **Responsibilities of Communications Personnel**

    6.1 Upon notification that a pursuit is in progress, communications personnel shall immediately advise a supervisor of essential information regarding the pursuit.

    6.2 Communications personnel shall also carry out the following responsibilities during the pursuit:

        6.2.1 Receive and record all incoming information on the pursuit and the pursued vehicle

        6.2.2 Control all radio communications and clear the radio channels of all non-emergency calls

        6.2.3 Perform relevant record and motor vehicle checks

        6.2.4 Coordinate and dispatch back-up assistance and air support units under the direction of the field supervisor

        6.2.5 When practical, notify neighboring jurisdictions when a pursuit may extend into their location. With that notification, the communications personnel should specify whether involvement is requested, as determined by the supervisor's directives.

7. **Responsibilities of Supervisor**

    7.1 After being notified of a department pursuit, a supervisor shall:

        7.1.1 Ensure proper radio channels and procedures are in use

        7.1.2 Ensure tactics conform with department policy

        7.1.3 Ensure only the necessary number of unit are involved

        7.1.4 Ensure allied agencies are notified

        7.1.5 Consider aborting the pursuit if cause exists

        7.1.6 Consider air support availability and practicality

    7.2 Upon termination of the pursuit, the supervisor shall:

        7.2.1 When practical, proceed to the termination point of the pursuit and provide appropriate assistance and supervision at the scene

        7.2.2 Ensure post-incident notifications

        7.2.3 Ensure the proper written reports are completed and forwarded to the section commander

---

Figure 6: Policy Format Using All Numbers

In addition, each page should have a header or footer that includes the name of the policy, effective date, and the page numbers. Including the policy's effective date in the header or footer ensures that all officers are using the most current version. (See Figure 7.)

Sample Policy—Police Use of Force	Date Reviewed September 25, 2003	5-1

Figure 7: Example of a Footer

Creating Cover Letters

Use a cover letter written on agency letterhead to introduce the policy. Such a letter conveys a sense of authority. The cover letter, an example of which is shown on the next page, should contain the following components:

- **Date**—The date on the letter identifies the distribution date for the policy.

- **Policy name, number, and status**—The policy name and number tells officers which policy is being updated. Identify whether it is a rough draft or the final version. (You may want to mark every page of draft policies with a DRAFT watermark to prevent confusion with the final version.)

- **Effective date**—If the policy is a final version, provide the effective date for the policy.

- **Policy being replaced**—If the new policy replaces an existing one, identify which policy is being replaced by title and number.

- **Training dates**—If the officers need to receive training on the new policy, provide them with a list of training dates.

- **Special instructions**—Include any special instructions you have for the officers. For example, you may want officers to remove previous versions of the policy from their notebooks and files. This can prevent situations such as the agency providing documentation in the deposition that the officers were trained in one version

Defensible Policies

of the policy, but then finds out that previous versions of a policy were found in the officers' notebooks.

(Agency Letterhead)

(Date)

TO: All officers and personnel

FR: (Name of Sheriff, Chief of Police or Director of Agency)

        (Title)

RE: (Policy)

Attached is **(a draft version/the final version)** of the **(new/amended)** policy for **(policy area)**, replacing the policy dated **(effective date of previous policy)**. It will go into effect **(effective date)**, the date by which all officers affected by the policy will have been trained to it. A copy of this policy should be kept in your personal notebook or file; all copies of the policy dated **(effective date of previous policy)** should be removed and destroyed.

Questions or concerns regarding the **(new/amended)** policy should be handled in the manner stipulated in Section **(Give section number where feedback process is covered)**.

Thank you.

Signature_____

Figure 8: Example of a Review Cover Letter

Conducting the Initial Review

After completing the first draft of the policy, distribute copies to each member of the policy group. The group needs to review the draft for technical accuracy and completeness. Use the review meeting to resolve any areas of conflict. While the group should be able to reach a general agreement, unresolved details can be addressed through the review process, which is discussed in the next chapter.

Discussion Questions

1. Who is the primary audience for a policy?

2. What steps should you take to ensure that the policy is written for the proper audience?

3. If a writer has not been appointed to the policy group, what is the advantage of using an agency specialist at this point in the development process?

4. What are the advantages of having a standardized format for all agency policies?

5. What should be addressed in a cover letter that accompanies a policy?

6. Why is it not crucial that the policy group be in complete agreement on the policy when the draft is completed?

Seven

Reviewing a Draft Policy

Objectives

In this chapter, you will learn how to do the following:

- *Understand why a policy draft should be reviewed*
- *Identify reviewers*
- *Maintain control of the review process*
- *Prepare a reviewer questionnaire*
- *Act on reviewer comments*

Once the policy group has evaluated the initial draft and has reached general consensus, it is time to send the policy to people outside the group for their input. To maximize the value of the review process, you need to ensure the following:

- Ensure that the appropriate people review the document at the appropriate time.
- Schedule sufficient time to review the policy.
- Use a review form to document feedback.
- Close the loop by informing the reviewer of why you didn't incorporate some of the feedback.

Importance of the Review Process

Reviews are important for the following reasons:

- **Build ownership among people affected by the policy.** Even if their ideas are not adopted, people will have a sense of ownership as long as they know those ideas were seriously considered.

- **Identify problems before the policy goes into effect.** Asking for feedback on a proposed policy enables you to get a better sense of its impact, and enables you to identify areas of concern that need to be addressed before the policy is finalized.

- **Improve the overall quality of the policy by incorporating a variety of viewpoints into a cohesive document.** The best policies are derived from discussions amongst a diverse group of people, each of whom brings a unique perspective and area of expertise to the process.

Keep in mind that soliciting people's opinion is not the same as giving them a veto. Just because one person disagrees with a particular aspect of a policy does not mean you have to change it. However, you do need to consider the feedback and document the reasons for your decision. It is easier to amend a policy that is under development than one that has already gone into effect.

Reviewers

When determining who should review a policy, consider the following:

- Include a representative sample of the people who will be affected by the policy.

- Assign primary reviewers from each functional area. They are then responsible for collecting and collating feedback from other people in their functional area. This will help manage the feedback and, at the same time, will foster discussion among the people affected by the policy.

- For volatile issues, increase the number of people involved, and include the agency's legal counsel and public relations representative in the review.

- Allow any agency employee who requests a copy to see it. Obviously, people who take the initiative feel they have a stake in the matter. Seeking out their input will go a long way toward building their sense of ownership in the final product.

Recommended Policy Reviewers

The information below describes the people who need to be involved in the policy review and explains why they should be involved.

- **Line officers and supervisors**—Since line officers and supervisors are the ones most affected by the policies, they should be allowed to comment on whether the proposed procedures will enable them to do their jobs in a safe, efficient manner. In a small agency, you might let everybody see it. This is probably not feasible in a large department, but you might want at least one representative from each division or subdivision.

- **Risk managers at other local agencies**—Because law enforcement interacts with so many segments of the community, it is important to ensure that the department's policies do not directly conflict with or contradict those of another local agency. Risk managers from other agencies will be familiar with their own policies and can provide valuable input into your agency's policies. Municipal leagues and other community associations are great resources for locating these reviewers. For example, Appendix A describes the process that the Michigan Municipal League has used successfully to develop model policies that members can use as templates for their developing own policies.

- **Other civic personnel with a stake in policy**— Government departments that oversee an agency or that provide a support function should have an opportunity to review a policy before it goes into effect. Such people may identify an issue or potential problem that could easily go unnoticed otherwise. You might also contact the heads of other law enforcement agencies; they are probably facing the same issues and may be addressing them in a different manner. As before, these agencies should be similar to yours in terms of size, community served, and resources available.

• **Members of the community**—Many law enforcement agencies are reluctant to allow the general public to participate in the internal processes of the department. However, a policy relating to any issue that impacts the larger community, especially if it is a highly explosive one, will be under scrutiny as soon as it is implemented. You would be better off getting community input before it becomes effective.

The advantages of involving people outside the agency are twofold. First, if they do participate, they will be more likely to support the final policy. If a problem occurs after implementation, the backlash might be less severe if the public has input into the process.

Second, soliciting outside opinions increases your defensibility. If a group protests a policy after an incident, your position will be stronger if you can show that you made a reasonable effort to get their input before the policy went into effect. Then, if they choose not to participate, you can truthfully say that you gave them an opportunity to contribute, but they declined to do so.

Controlling the Review Process

Because many people within your agency need to review a policy before it goes into effect, you need to keep a log of who has each copy of the policy. Doing so will help you to follow up on comments as well. To track the review copies, number each copy of a draft being reviewed and keep a log of who receives it, the date they receive it, and the date it is returned with their comments. See Figure 9 for a sample log.

Log of Agency Reviewers

Policy:_____   Draft #:_____

Due Date of Review:_____

Name	Rank/Division	Phone # and Email	Date Out	Date In
1.				
2.				
3.				
4.				
5.				
6.				
7.				
8.				
9.				
10.				

Figure 9: Sample Review Log for Agency Reviewers

Keep a log for outside reviewers, too. However, require these reviewers to request a copy in writing. The request should include a clear statement that the reviewers understand that this is not a "live" policy; it is only a draft under consideration. An additional statement should indicate their understanding that, while recommendations will be considered, they may not be adopted. Figure 10 shows an example of an outsider log. Figure 11 shows a request letter that external reviewers can use to request copies of policies.

To further protect yourself, place "DRAFT" on every page of a review policy. This helps avoid confusion when the final policy is issued. You do not want officers or the public to mistake a draft policy that details one set of procedures for the actual one that calls for another.

Log of Outside Reviewers

Policy:_____   Draft #:_____

Due Date of Review:_____

Name	Address	Phone # and Email	Date Out	Date In
1.				
2.				
3.				
4.				
5.				
6.				
7.				
8.				
9.				
10.				

Figure 10: Sample Review Log for External Reviewers

(Group or Association Letterhead, if applicable)

(Date)

TO: (Name of Person in Charge of Policy Group)
FR: (Name of Reviewer)
        (Address)
        (Phone #)
RE: Review of (Policy)

I would like to review and provide input on the policy being developed to address the area of (**Policy Area**).

I understand that the version of the policy that I will review is only a draft and that my input will be evaluated and considered by the Policy Resource Group. The Policy Resource Group will decide whether my input is incorporated into the final policy.

I further understand that my written comments must be submitted to (**Name of Document Coordinator**) by (**Due Date**) in order for my comments to be considered.

Signature:_____

Figure 11: Sample Letter for External Review Requests

Finally, schedule a review period for all reviewers, both inside and outside the agency. Review deadlines enable you to continue moving forward with the process once the comment period is over. If you do not give deadlines, the policy development process will stall. Make it clear that written comments must be returned by a certain date for the policy group to consider them. Setting such a limit gives you an additional measure of protection. If reviewers do not return their comments on time, you can truthfully say you gave them an opportunity to be heard, but they did not act on it.

Of course, you must allot a reasonable amount of time. Typically, a review period lasts at least one week, but not more than three weeks, and is included in the overall schedule for the policy development project. This time frame gives reviewers enough time to read through a policy, to evaluate the procedures being proposed, to consider the consequences of them, and to generate a written response stating their positions. If you give too much time, reviewers tend to forget about the review.

Documenting Reviewer Comments

As with the preliminary issues list and the log, you need to document the review comments, as well as the decisions made based on those comments. This is best done using a questionnaire. A standardized form helps reviewers by giving them a format for voicing their recommendations. It also helps the policy group by structuring responses so they are easier to evaluate and compare. At the same time, you can use a series of pointed questions to gather information about issues that need more research.

There are a few things to keep in mind when compiling a questionnaire. You can find a sample of a reviewer questionnaire on page 69.

- **Base questions on the needs established by the policy group.** Obviously, the policy was developed to meet the needs identified early in the development process.

Structure the review questions to find out how well the draft policy meets those needs.

- **Use open-ended questions.** Questions should do more than elicit "yes/no" responses. Open-ended questions require people to explain their position rather than simply saying they agree or disagree. If you do use a simple response question, ask for more information, such as "If your answer is 'no,' please explain."

- **Use a structured form.** Provide spaces for answers on the questionnaire. The spaces allow you to steer the reviewer toward the areas you think are most important. If one question allots twice as much room for a response as another, it will be clear that the first question carries more weight.

- **Address issues the policy group could not resolve.** Ask questions about areas where the policy group still disagrees. By learning what other people think about those issues, the policy group might be able to resolve the disagreement.

- **Allot space for overall comments.** Give reviewers a chance to comment on the policy in general and raise individual concerns. Such concerns might identify a problem the policy group had not thought of.

- **Require authentication.** Somewhere on the form, you should have space for the reviewer's signature, the date the comments were made, and contact information, should the policy group needs clarification or additional information.

Reviewer Questionnaire

Policy:_____   Draft # _____   Copy #:____

Date out:_____   Date due in:_____

Reviewer Name:_____

Address:_____

Phone #:_____   Email address:_____

Areas of Focus:

Please address the following areas, using separate sheets of paper if additional space is needed.

    1. Does the breakdown of components seem logical? What other components should be added? What should be deleted?

    2. Do the steps advocated in the each component seem appropriate? If not, which ones are causes for concern and how could they be adjusted?

    3. How could safety be enhanced?

General comments:

Signature:_____   **Date:**_____

Figure 12: Reviewer Questionnaire

Acting on Reviewer Comments

The reviewers should submit their comments to the coordinator for the document repository. The coordinator then provides copies of the comments to everyone in the policy group.

While you do not need to make every change that is suggested, the policy group does need to evaluate and discuss each comment. If the group agrees with the comment, the change is incorporated into the policy. If a change is not made, document the reasons for rejecting the idea and notify the reviewer who presented the idea.

If the policy is modified extensively, it might be necessary to prepare a second draft for review. This will likely require an adjustment to the policy implementation schedule. However, it is better to delay a policy's effective date than to rush one out if the policy does not adequately address the problems it was created to solve.

If the changes are minor, the writer can produce a final version of the policy and submit it to the policy group for final review and approval. Once the policy group approves the updated version, the policy can be published and distributed.

Discussion Questions

1. What is a policy review? Why have a review?

2. Who are the people who should serve as reviewers?

3. What determines how many reviewers should be used?

4. What are the advantages of having selected members of the community serve as reviewers?

5. What steps should you take to keep control of the review process?

6. Why should all reviewers have a time limit for completing their reviews?

7. What guidelines should be used when putting together a reviewer questionnaire?

8. Under what circumstances would reviewer comments lead you to prepare an additional draft for a second round of reviews?

Eight

Training to Policy

Objectives

In this chapter, you will learn how to do the following:

- *Develop a defensible program for policy certification*
- *Understand training methods and learning styles*
- *Develop a defensible program for re-certification*

As the *Canton v. Harris* decision shows, training programs are a critical part of ensuring that your policies are defensible. While the facts in *Canton* and the examples used by the Supreme Court to explain its decision were about specific skills officers must have, the case could very well apply to policies, as well. After a policy has been developed, it must be implemented in a defensible manner.

Certifying to Policy

In the past, agencies rarely had a systematic plan to ensure that the officers truly understood what was expected of them. Most agencies exposed their officers to the policies by handing them a policy manual on the officers' first day, then telling them to read the manual and to sign a declaration stating that they understood the policies. This is the equivalent of issuing officers weapons, and having them sign a sheet stating that they know how to use them.

Today, agencies must certify that their officers understand policies. Certification ensures the following:

- Authenticates that officers have been exposed to a policy.

- Ensures that the officers have had an opportunity to ask questions about a policy.

- Ensures that officers agree to be bound by a policy.

These training and documentation requirements differentiate certification from previous practices. Certifying the officers requires the following tasks:

1. Issue the policy to all officers and instruct them to read it. Use a cover letter to inform that this is the final version of the policy. Otherwise, they might mistake it for another draft.

2. Schedule a question and answer session so that officers have an opportunity to ask questions. You can handle this in one of the following ways:

   o *An in-service program.* The person presenting the program reviews each component and then provides the line officers with the opportunity to ask questions.

   o *Presentation during roll call.* Set aside time at the beginning of each shift to discuss a component or two and to answer any related questions. Most policies can be addressed in this manner within a few days. Since officers are already required to attend the roll call, no additional cost is associated with this type of training.

3. Ensure that the sessions are conducted by someone who understands the policy. You do not want a supervisor or someone else to say to the officers, "If it were up to me, we wouldn't do it this way. But this is what the Chief wants, so....." This conveys the message that the policy will not be stringently enforced. Without enforcement, a policy will quickly break down, exposing the agency to liability and creating a system where custom instead of process determines policy.

4. Consider testing the officers' understanding of the policy. Make the test fairly straight-forward, giving the

facts of an incident or two and asking questions about how the policy would apply. This is a good idea for policies that are of particular concern to the agency or to the community.

5. Document that each officer attended the training session and have them sign a declaration stating that they understand and will abide by the policy. Include the date the policy becomes effective, followed by a clear statement that the officers understand they will be bound by the terms of the policy as of that time. (See Figure 13.)

Policy Endorsement

(Date)

Officer: (Name)
       (Rank/Badge #)
       (Division)

RE: (Policy)

I, the undersigned officer, have been given a copy of the **(new/amended)** policy for **(policy area)**. This copy of the policy replaces the policy dated **(effective date of previous policy)**. I have read the **(new/amended)** policy, understand it, and have had an opportunity to ask for clarifications regarding it.

I understand that the **(new/amended)** policy will go into effect on **(effective date)**. I also understand that, as of that date, I will be required to abide by its provisions and will be held accountable to it.

Signature of Officer:_____

Date:_____

Signature of Supervisor:_____

Date:_____

Figure 13: Sample Certification and Policy Endorsement

Presenting the Training

When presenting the training, it is important for the trainer to believe in the policy and to emphasize the requirements of the policy, while maintaining a positive attitude. Strive to give officers the impression that the policy is meant to support them. Reinforce that they can provide feedback about the policy, but they must comply with the policy as long as it's in effect.

There will always be one or two officers who resist change. The trainer needs to be prepared to defuse their objections and arguments by fully understanding the issues and benefits of the policy. Other officers will be watching. If the trainer conveys the impression that less than full compliance will be tolerated, the policy will fail.

During the training, give the officers information about the proper channels for providing feedback on the policy. This will help build ownership among the officers. You do not want them to view the policy as just an effort to protect upper management from liability exposure.

If a significant number of officers are unhappy about the policy, assume a problem exists that needs attention. Address their concerns by re-evaluating their previous input or by conducting additional research, and consider delaying the implementation until such issues are resolved. If the policy group determines that the policy should remain as is, explain why the policy was written the way it was. Officers do not have to completely agree with a policy, but they do need to understand why it is as it is. If they know the underlying reasons behind the policy, they will be more likely to accept it.

Learning Style

The following three learning styles indicate how people best receive information (Rose, 1987):

- **Visual**—These learners tend to prefer pictures, demonstrations, and other visual stimuli. They may easily remember faces, but they have more difficulty with names and may be easily distracted by movement.

- **Auditory**—These learners tend to prefer dialog and conversation and written or verbal instructions, and may remember names better than faces. Background noise and other sounds can be very distracting.

- **Kinesthetic/tactile**—These learners tend to prefer experiential learning where they can role play or try out the activity. They may remember what they did with someone more than the person's name or physical characteristics. Surrounding activities may be distracting to them.

In addition, individuals have preferred ways of processing information, which fall into the following four categories (Felder, 2004):

- **Active vs. reflective**—Active learners need to do something with the information in order to understand it. Reflective learners need to think about the information in order to understand it.

- **Sensing vs. intuitive**—Sensing learners need concrete facts and data, and prefer to use established methods for analyzing the information. Lack of logical and sequential connection may make sensing learners uncomfortable. Intuitive learners tend to make "leaps" in connecting information conceptually, are comfortable with abstractions, and dislike rote memorization.

- **Visual vs. verbal**—Just as with the visual and auditory learning styles described above, visual learners prefer seeing pictures, flowcharts, demonstrations, or diagrams. Auditory learners prefer listening and discussing the topic.

- **Sequential vs. global**—Sequential learners need to receive information in logical steps, and to have an understanding of how the pieces connect with each other. Even if they don't understand the "big picture", these learners can still make use of the information. Global learners must understand the "big picture" before they can absorb and understand the details. Once global learners make the connection, however, they often quickly solve complex problems or derive novel solutions from the information.

While everyone has a preferred learning style, no one uses a single approach exclusively. The best training accommodates each learning style by creatively incorporating activities and presentation materials, so that everyone has an opportunity to learn using their strongest style.

Acceptable Training Methods

There are three main methods for training officers on policies. The first is **training with video**. Incorporating a video into the training helps to ensure consistency. Someone will still need to discuss the policy with the officers and answer their questions, but a video can present the various policy components. The advantages of video include the following:

- **Standardizes the presentation of policy.** A videotape guarantees that the policy will be presented to every officer in exactly the same way. Video eliminates a problem that may exist if one supervisor's presentation skills are not as good as others within the department.

- **Establishes authority and credibility.** A video enables the chief or some other high-level officer to present the policy to all in-service programs or to all shifts. Even if the chief does not present the entire training program, he or she may be able to provide an introduction, which reinforces the importance of the policy.

- **Gives more control over the presentation.** You can view the video before showing it to your officers to make sure it achieves all of the agency's objectives and places the proper emphasis on the key points.

- **Can be used in re-certification programs.** When it comes time to re-certify officers, the video can be shown again, ensuring a continued standard of training. (This is discussed further in "Re-Certifying to Policy" on page 78.)

- **Serves as documentation of training.** If your implementation procedure is ever questioned, you can produce the video to demonstrate how the policy was presented.

The biggest disadvantage to video is the cost of creating a professional product. In addition, producing a video may require more time than developing a slide program that the supervisors then use to conduct the training. While you gain in consistency, you lose flexibility.

A second type of training is **instructor-led training**. The advantage of instructor-led training is that officers can directly ask questions, and the instructor can provide additional examples or use role playing to clarify or to illustrate a key idea in the policy. Instructor-led training can be tailored more easily to the needs of individual officers.

Typically, instructor-led training is less expensive than video, and more flexible, in that instructors can easily modify the training if the policy is updated or needs to be changed.

The primary disadvantage is that the quality of the training can be highly variable, depending on the skill of the individual instructor. There are solutions to this issue:

- Provide train-the-trainer sessions to ensure that all the instructors fully understand the policy and that their presentation skills are up to par.

- Certify and designate certain team members as agency trainers. They are then responsible for conducting the training for all the officers in the division or agency.

A third training option is **self-study and test**. This option is the least expensive, but it is also the least defensible. In this scenario, officers receive the policy manual, read it, and then take a test that evaluates their understanding. Once they pass the test, the officers sign a declaration of understanding.

The biggest disadvantage of this training method is that it is difficult to ensure that all officers truly understand the policy, and to ensure that the training is consistent. Because officers tend to be action-oriented people, it may be difficult for them to just sit and read the policy manual. In addition, this method does not provide the officers an opportunity to ask questions.

Most agencies find that a blend of video, instructor-led training, and self-study provides the best training opportunity.

Re-Certifying to Policy

An important component of any training program is re-certification, which simply means proving that officers still fully understand the policy. Re-certification should occur as often as necessary to ensure understanding and compliance with the policy, and should be scheduled at regular intervals, such as every six months, once a year, or every two years. The timing of a re-certification program depends on the policy and the particular issue it addresses. It might also become apparent if an incident occurs that reveals a policy needs to be reinforced, or when the policy is modified.

Re-certification means repeating the original training, incorporating any modifications to the policy. Present the policy to the officers. If no amendments have been made, you can simply re-run the video or redo the presentation used in the initial training. If the policy has been modified, the video or presentation can be edited to reflect those changes. Provide officers the opportunity to ask questions, and then have them sign the declaration stating that they understand the policy and will abide by it. If necessary, you can re-test them on the policy.

Re-certification also provides an important channel for feedback, giving you an opportunity to find out what officers think about a policy's effectiveness. For instance, you might say something like, "You have been working with this policy for some time now. Are you having any problems with it? If so, what are they and how would you recommend that we correct them?" Besides providing valuable information, this opportunity will enhance the officers' sense of ownership. As long as they continue to see policy as a tool for them, they will be more likely to abide by it.

Discussion Questions

1. What is meant by certifying an officer to policy? How is this done?

2. What are the advantages to using videotaped presentations of policy in training?

3. What learning style do most line officers have?

4. What must be covered in a line officer endorsement of policy?

5. When might it be a good idea to use a test as a component of policy training?

6. What is meant by re-certifying to policy? How often should it take place?

7. How can the re-certification process serve as a channel of policy feedback?

Notes

Nine

Enforcing Policy

Objectives

In this chapter, you will learn how to do the following:

- *Understand the crucial role supervisors play in policy enforcement*
- *Base agency reports on policies*

$\mathbf{M}$any good policies fail due to lack of enforcement. Even the best policy will fail without a mechanism to document and ensure officer compliance. Effective supervision, coupled with comprehensive programs of reporting and reviewing incidents, is the key to successful policy enforcement.

Supervisors' Role

Most line officers do not start out with the intention of deviating from policy. Instead, they may make modifications for convenience if a policy is not being strictly enforced. If supervisors do not correct such deviations immediately, the officers, and possibly the courts, will construe these deviations as acceptable. On the other hand, if line officers clearly understand that a policy is being taken seriously, the policy and the procedures advocated in it will quickly become the accepted practice of the agency.

Supervisors are the most important assets in policy enforcement because they observe the daily actions of the line officers. When observing those actions, supervisors can determine if officers are conforming to the policies and procedures. Supervisors can immediately reinforce positive responses, as well as correct non-compliance. By using the policy as a guideline, supervisors also can gather solid information for objective performance appraisals.

In addition, on-site observations allow supervisors to judge how well line officers perform the tasks prescribed by policy. If officers routinely fall short of expectations, supervisors can identify areas where the officers may need additional training to perform the tasks correctly.

Supervisors can also evaluate the effectiveness of the policy itself. By seeing it being put into practice on the street, they will likely be the first ones to identify areas where the policy is weak. This unique vantage point places supervisors in the best position to recommend changes that increase safety and/or efficiency.

Building Supervisory Ownership

If supervisors have input into policies and feel a sense of ownership, they will ensure that the officers abide by the policy. If supervisors do not support a policy, they may simply choose not to enforce it. You can build a sense of ownership among the supervisors in the following ways:

- **Include supervisors in policy development**—Using supervisors in the development process helps ensure that the policy becomes a useful tool for both them and their officers. As an administrator, never hand supervisors a finished policy document and say, "This is the policy of this agency; it is your job to enforce it." That approach leads to a confrontational environment, especially if supervisors view the policy as something not grounded in street reality.

- **Involve supervisors in policy training**—Since they oversee line officer compliance, supervisors should be the ones answering policy questions raised by the officers during training. Having supervisors train their officers gives them an increased responsibility for the policy. It also helps establish authority. In the minds of line officers, a supervisor who participates in policy training advocates that policy, which conveys the impression that the policy will be strictly enforced. Of course, before supervisors can conduct the training for line officers, you must first provide a separate training session for supervisors.

- **Support supervisors**—A major component of enforcement is discipline. By supporting the disciplinary recommendations of supervisors, you give them the necessary authority to bring wayward officers back into compliance and to keep other officers focused. To alleviate potential conflicts, include discipline as a component of the policy. If the consequences of non-conformance are clearly spelled out, supervisors will know what action to take, and line officers will know what action to expect.

Reports

Another important aspect of enforcement is reporting. Design agency reports to capture information in the context of policy:

- **Ask detailed questions about an incident.** Use the procedures from the policy as the basis of those questions. That way you know whether the policy was followed and get a sense of how the policy functioned in that particular incident.

- **Keep forms simple and easy to use.** Doing so will increase the likelihood that the reports are completed consistently, correctly, and thoroughly, and will make it easier to analyze the information.

Basing reports on policy also helps reinforce the policy. By requiring officers to think along policy lines when filling out reports, they will begin to view incidents in terms of policy. If officers know they will have to document why they continued pursuing a fleeing suspect in a speeding car, or made an arrest during a domestic violence call, they will consciously examine those reasons as events unfold, increasing the likelihood that those decisions will be based on the proper guidelines.

Components of Effective Report Forms

Forms can be fairly simple and still provide the essential information. At the end of this chapter are examples of forms designed to work with a detailed policy on emergency vehicle operations:

- Incident report form designed to capture all of the facts of the incident. (See pages 88-90.)

- Summary sheet where the officer provides detailed facts about the incident. (See page 91.)

Notice that the summary sheet is divided into three main areas (initiation, continuation and termination) so that the officer can address key components of a pursuit policy. Each component asks questions that stimulate the officer's thought process related to the policy concerns.

Supervisors also need an incident reporting form. This form gathers essentially the same type of information as the officers' forms, but from the supervisors' perspective. (See page 92.) This form includes the following sections:

- Analysis of an officer's version of events

- Evaluation of officer compliance with the policy

- Description of any specific deviant actions, including a detailed report of any consequences resulting from them

- Summary where the supervisor describes their overall impressions of the incident, including issues with the policy itself. Encourage every supervisor to critique the policy and raise any issue that could lead to a policy adjustment

- Training recommendations, if supervisors think non-compliance was due to the officer's lack of understanding of the policy

Post-Incident Reviews

A final aspect of enforcement is the post-incident review. During the review, the line officer and supervisor discuss the incident and compare the actions during the incident to the policy directives that guide those actions. Ensure that officers understand that reviews are intended as objective evaluations to ensure safety and efficiency, and are not intended to be punitive. Officers must have the opportunity to describe their impressions of the incident and to voice any concerns that they have about the policy as a result of the incident.

Schedule post-incident reviews as soon as possible after each incident occurs, so that the incident is still fresh in everyone's mind, and make the review standard procedure.

Importance of Post-Incident Reviews

Post-incident reviews are important for several reasons, which are explained in the following sections.

- **Reinforces policy**—A review enables you to understand the officer's thought processes as events unfolded. If decisions were based on policy, you can reinforce that behavior. If policy was not the guiding force, provide constructive feedback so that the officer will make a better decision the next time. With consistent feedback, officers will quickly understand what is expected of them.

- **Strengthens accountability**—Officers must know where they stand. When you make it a practice to discuss each incident with the officers involved, they immediately understand whether they acted properly or improperly. Such reviews ensure that officers know they will be held accountable for their actions. In most cases, officers know whether they stayed within the limits of policy. If they did and receive positive reinforcement, they will likely continue to do so. On the other hand, if the officer did not follow policy and is not corrected, he or she may conclude their actions were acceptable.

- **Allows for a critique of the agency**—Allow officers to discuss their concerns about the agency, the incident, or the policy. This is especially important if they believe the agency did not provide the tools or support they needed to get the job done in the most effective manner.

- **Allows for a critique of the policy**—A review gives both the supervisor and the line officer an opportunity to discuss how well the policy worked during an incident. When it comes to the effectiveness of policy, the primary consideration is safety. Encourage officers to raise any issue that compromises safety, and to present any ideas that enhance safety.

- **Leads to a continued sense of ownership by line officers**—Ideally, the review provides an objective forum where the line officer can discuss the incident and its associated policy. If officers believe their input is valued they will feel a greater ownership of the policy. As long as officers continue to see a policy as a tool designed for their use and safety, they will be more likely to stay within its guidelines.

Post-Incident Review Process

As soon as practical after an incident, the supervisor needs to schedule the review. In preparing for the review, the supervisor reads the officer's reports to determine if any questions still exist, or if any responses are unclear. If discrepancies exist between the officer's and the supervisor's accounts of events, they should be resolved during this meeting.

A review needs to be a *mutual* exchange of information. both sides need to provide feedback about all facets of an incident. If officers do not get an opportunity to discuss their own concerns, they will view debriefings as inquisitions designed primarily to blame them for anything that may have gone wrong. This attitude significantly reduces the effectiveness of the policy and of the review.

Using a standard agenda or a debriefing form will help to guide the discussion and to ensure that the review remains as objective as possible.

After the review, the supervisor documents that it took place, summarizing the highlights (especially if they clarify what happened in the incident), and then forwards this information up the chain of command, along with the other reports of the incident. (See page 93 for an sample post-incident review form.)

All supervisors need to understand the importance of this process because of their roles in policy enforcement and analysis. If supervisors do not conduct thorough reviews and do not pass on complete information, a policy cannot remain current and cannot continue to fit the needs of the officers, the agency, or the community. The communication loop is discussed more fully in the next chapter.

Discussion Questions

1. Why must line officers who deviate from policy be brought back into compliance immediately?

2. How are supervisors the key to policy enforcement?

3. What steps can you take to build supervisory ownership in a policy?

4. Why should reports be based on policy?

5. Why should post-incident reviews be standard procedures?

6. How should a post-incident review be conducted?

Pursuit Incident Report

General Pursuit Information

Your Name:	Supervisor:

Division/Detachment:	Names of other officers involved:

Unit #'s of other vehicles involved::	Vehicle # involved	Description of your vehicle:
		□ Marked □ Semi-marked □ Unmarked □ Other (specify) _____

Date of incident	Time pursuit began	Time pursuit ended	Elapsed time

Location pursuit began	Location pursuit ended	Distance covered	Est. max speed

Suspect

Suspect Name:	_____
Gender:	**Age range:**
□ Male □ Female	□ Under 18 □ 36-45 □ 18-25 □ 46-55 □ 26-35 □ 56+

Description of Suspect Vehicle

License	Year	Make	Model	Color

Figure 14: Sample Incident Report (page 1)

Environmental conditions

Weather (choose one)	Light (choose one)	Road (choose all that apply)
☐ Clear	☐ Daylight	☐ Dry
☐ Rain	☐ Dawn/Dusk	☐ Wet
☐ Snow	☐ Dark with streetlight	☐ Snow/Icy
☐ Fog/Mist	☐ Dark without streetlight	Construction/Repair
☐ Other (specify)		☐ Other (specify)
_____		_____
		☐

Area (choose all that apply)	Vehicular traffic (choose one)	Pedestrian traffic (choose one)
☐ Residential	☐ None	☐ None
☐ School	☐ Light	☐ Light
☐ Playground	☐ Moderate	☐ Moderate
☐ Commercial/Industrial	☐ Heavy	☐ Heavy
☐ Expressway		
☐ Other (specify)		

Initiation

Reason for initiation	Emergency Equipment deployed
☐ Traffic violation	Lights on (time)_____
☐ Criminal offense (Specify)	Siren on (time)_____
_____	
☐ Neighboring agency requested assistance	
_____	

Termination

How terminated	If no apprehension, indicate reason
☐ Suspect pulled over	☐ Suspect identified
☐ Officer opted to terminate	☐ Pursuit became unsafe
☐ Officer directed to terminate	☐ Officer's vehicle malfunctioned
☐ Officer used force to terminate	☐ Lost sight of suspect vehicle
	☐ Other (specify)
	_____

Force was authorized by supervisor	Emergency equipment off
☐ Yes	Lights off (time) _____
☐ No	Siren off (time)_____

Force used to terminate pursuit (specify)	Firearm discharged
☐ Boxed in	☐ Yes
☐ Road spikes	☐ No
☐ Forced off road	
☐ PIT	
☐ Roadblock	
☐ Rammed	

Figure 15: Sample Incident Report (page 2)

Termination (continued):

Suspect apprehended	Condition of suspect
□ Yes □ No	□ Normal □ Impaired (specify) ————————————————
Force used to subdue suspect and other occupants	**Were you in control at scene of termination?**
□ No force used—suspect did not resist □ Force required (specify type of force used) ———————————— ————————————————	□ Yes □ No Who took control? ————————————————
# of occupants in vehicle	**Time you relinquish control**

Allied Agencies

Allied Agencies Involved?	For each allied agency
□ Yes (specify) ———————————— □ No	Number of vehicles involved———————— Names of officers: ———————————————— ———————————————— ————————————————
Reason for involvement	**Did you request allied assistance?**
□ Pursuit initiate in allied jurisdiction □ Pursuit crossed allied jurisdiction	□ Yes □ No

Result of Pursuit

Police	Suspect vehicle and occupants	Third Parties
Damage to vehicle □ Yes □ No # of people injured——— # of fatalities———	*Damage to vehicle* □ Yes □ No # of people injured——— # of fatalities———	*Property damage* □ Yes □ No # of people injured——— # of fatalities———
For all injuries **Emergency aid requested**	**Time of request**	**Time of aid arrival**
□ Yes □ No		

Figure 16: Sample Incident Report (page 3)

Summary Sheet

Date:_____

	You	Supervisor
Name		
Rank		
Badge Number		
Division/Detachment		

Incident

Date of incident	Name of Suspect

Description of Suspect's vehicle

License	Year	Make	Model	Color

Initiation

- Why did you initiate this pursuit?

Continuation

- How long did the pursuit last?
- Why did you pursue the suspect for that length of time?

Termination

- How was the pursuit terminated?
- Why did you terminate it in that manner?
- If you used force to subdue the suspect. why was that force necessary?
- If there was a third party injury or property damage, what was the nature of the incident and how did it happen?

Signature:_____

Note: Attach a copy of your pursuit incident report.

Figure 17: Incident Summary Sheet

General Incident Report
(Supervisor)

Date:_____

	Supervisor	Line Officer
Name		
Rank		
Badge Number		
Division/Detachment		

Incident ID:	Date of incident:

Facts of incident as reported by Line Officer:

Supervisorial response:

☐   I concur with the facts as reported by Line Officer.

☐   I DO NOT concur with the facts as reported by Line Officer. (State what your version of the facts are, indicating how they differ from Line Officer version. Use a separate sheet, if necessary.)

Supervisorial analysis:

☐   Line Officer abided by the governing policy for this incident.

☐   Line Officer DID NOT abide by the governing policy for this incident. (State what deviations took place and any mitigating reasons for such deviations. Use a separate sheet, if necessary.)

Recommendations:

Signature:_____

Note: Attach a copy of all relevant documents and reports.

Figure 18: Sample Supervisor's Report

Post-Incident Review

Date: _____

	Supervisor	Line Officer
Name		
Rank		
Badge Number		
Division/Detachment		

Critique of Incident

Type of Incident:	Date of incident:

Facts of incident:
(Attach copies of reports by Line Officer and Supervisor.) If new information has come to light, indicate in space below.

Line Officer wants to add to or clarify any statements or fact put forth in his/her reporting of this incident.
☐ Yes. Attach comments on separate sheet.
☐ No

Supervisor wants to add to or clarify any statements or facts put forth in his/her reporting of this incident.
☐ Yes. Attach comments on separate sheet.
☐ No

Line Officer's response to Supervisor's recommendation. (Comments are encouraged and can be made in space provided or on an separate sheet.)
☐ Agrees
☐ Disagrees
☐ Prefers not to comment

Figure 19: Sample Post-Incident Review Form

Notes

Ten

Conducting Ongoing Analysis

Objectives

In this chapter, you will learn how to do the following:

* *Get feedback*
* *Understand the role of a policy risk manager*
* *Act on policy feedback*

As shown by the case of *Tennessee v. Garner*, a policy needs to be re-evaluated frequently. New technologies affect the way we operate. Court decisions create new standards. Operational issues on the streets of your community may change. Any or all of these situations may result in a policy that no longer meets your officers' needs. To keep a policy current, you need a systematic process of evaluation and review.

Closing the Loop

This process begins by establishing a channel to bring information from the line officers to the administration. In effect, you need to "close the loop". You may have obtained input from supervisors and line officers during the development phase, but you still issued the final policy directives and mandated that officers participate in training programs on them. Now, you need to bring information back up to you. You need to establish a channel for assessing the policy's effectiveness and officer's response capabilities. You will then be able to demonstrate that the agency is in a continual state of policy administration and risk management, documenting that either the problem has been solved, or that it needs further attention for which you can take additional documented action.

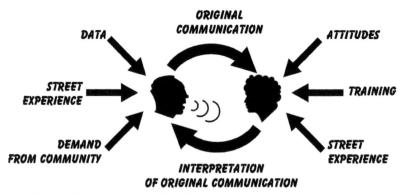

Figure 20: Communication Feedback Loop

Using multiple methods of collecting feedback increases the likelihood that you will identify areas that need to be updated before they become a problem. When you request feedback, it is critical that you "close the loop" by communicating action items and decisions that arose from that feedback. There are several ways to encourage and collect feedback, as described in the following sections.

Reviews

Make the post-incident review a standard practice and ensure officers understand that this meeting is an opportunity for them to provide feedback on the policy's effectiveness, and to identify the need for resources and training. Encourage input by making the review meeting a positive and constructive experience.

Suggestion Box

Suggestion boxes provide a way for anyone in the agency to provide feedback on the spur of the moment. Conveniently and prominently placed boxes remind employees that their feedback is expected and appreciated. Periodically, posting a list of the suggestions and what's being done about them also fosters a sense of ownership and encourages participation.

Periodic Surveys

Surveys can be a great way to solicit feedback on issues that you are concerned about. For large agencies, you may want to develop a random survey that goes out to a percentage of the employees. For smaller agencies, you may want to survey everyone. Developing a regular schedule for disseminating surveys and then posting the resulting action items and decisions encourages a culture of feedback. This demonstrates the administration really does want input and wants to ensure the best work environment for everyone.

Annual Policy Reviews

Regular reviews of existing policies ensures that issues are caught early and policies are kept up to date. During the review, research related court decisions, technology updates, and other information that may affect a policy. (The checklist on the next page can help you assess the impact of new technology.)

Regular reviews also gives officers and supervisors a greater sense of ownership. When officers know their input is desired and will be considered, they are more likely to contribute willingly to the policy process. They are also more likely to see policy as a tool designed for their use, possibly even viewing it as a safety net put in place for their protection. Providing multiple channels for feedback builds a culture of mutual respect and information exchange that is vital for team cohesion and success.

The policy group should also remain engaged in the feedback process. For the first few months a policy is in place, the group should seek regular feedback on how the policy is working and be prepared to make adjustments. From time to time, the group can also address the policy's current state relating to court decisions impacting it. One way of keeping the policy group engaged in the process is to assign employees to the policy group for a specified period of time or for a particular type of policy. Doing so helps to maintain continuity.

Incorporating New Technologies into Policies

The following checklist is intended to assist you in evaluating your existing policies and procedures when introducing new technologies into the agency.

1. Review the existing policies and procedures for similar technologies.
   a. Does the policy work for the new technology without revision?
   b. Can you adapt the policy to the new technology?
   c. What changes do you need to make?
2. Review the existing policies and procedures that apply to the same areas of law enforcement. For example, pepper spray, bean bags, and tasers all fall under non-lethal uses of force.
   a. What changes do you need to make to include the new technology?
   b. Do you need a separate policy for the new technology?
3. Identify any areas that are not currently covered by existing policies, but which are impacted by the new technology.
   a. Do these areas need a policy?
   b. Should there be a policy even without the new technology?
   c. How does the new technology impact the need for a policy?
4. Perform a cost/ benefit analysis to determine if the problems solved by the technology outweigh any new problems introduced by the technology. For example, tasers provide an additional, non-lethal method of controlling a suspect, but can have serious medical consequences.
   a. Do the benefits outweigh the costs or complications associated with using a technology?
   b. What problems does the technology solve and what problems does it create or worsen?
5. Identify ways to mitigate the risks associated with a new technology.
   a. What are the potential risks for using the new technology and how can the agency prevent negative consequences?
   b. How can line officers ensure safety when using the new technology?
   c. What additional training will be needed for the new technology?
   d. How will the training be incorporated into existing training programs?
6. Consider setting up a pilot program to test how the new technology will work with your department. Pilot programs enable you to identify problem areas and make adjustments before introducing the technology to the whole department or agency.
   a. What issues arise during the pilot period?
   b. What metrics determine success?
   c. What is the schedule for expanding the program or making a "no-go" decision?
   d. What policies are impacted by the pilot program? What interim procedures apply to the pilot program?

In addition, establishing a state or regional organization where agency representatives can exchange information helps to ensure your agency's policies are complete and meet applicable statutes. Such forums formalize the process of exchanging information among colleagues, as well as providing a broader perspective of experiences and issues that may not be currently addressed in your agency.

For example, MML has implemented an exemplary program called Law Enforcement Action Forum (LEAF) where Michigan agencies can exchange ideas and work together to develop model policies that can be adapted for specific agency needs. (These model policies are intended as templates to assist the member agencies in formulating policy, but are not intended to be used verbatim.)

Assigning an Agency Risk Manager

Most lawsuits stem from high-risk, low-frequency events. While they do not happen often, such events can affect an entire agency when they do occur. This book advocates preparing for those incidents by managing policies using sound risk management practices. One way to add substance and accountability to this process is to assign one person to function as a risk manager for the agency.

The risk manager monitors all agency operations and is responsible for the entire policy process. This individual works to identify areas where new or different policy might be required. For existing policies, the risk manager ensures any given policy meets the agency needs and continues to meet those needs over time. While decisions should not be made autocratically, the risk manager should have the authority to step in at any point to keep all policy-related activities functioning effectively, and to get the ball rolling in areas where new policies may be needed.

In addition to facilitating agency activities, the risk manager acts as the conduit for all information exchanged between the policy group and the general public. Part of this responsibility includes tracking and responding to community complaints filed with the agency, as well as decisions handed down by the courts. This effort will help keep the policy aligned with the expectations of the community and within the standards being established through the judicial system. The agency risk manager also acts as liaison and coordinates with any outside risk managers from insurance carriers, risk pools, or other organizations that may be working with the agency.

Responsibilities of the Agency Risk Manager

Each agency needs to determine how the position best fits within the organization, but the following list provides some general skills and responsibilities:

- **Ensures that policy directives are distributed properly.** All officers who will be affected by a new or revised policy should receive a copy of it.

- **Monitors the training programs to ascertain their effectiveness.** Upon completion, the officers must be able to understand the policy being issued, especially in terms of what is expected of them and when it goes into effect.

- **Tracks agency operations.** This activity will yield objective evidence of whether a policy is having the desired effect. At the same time, it might point to areas that may require the development of a new policy, a clarification of existing directives, or additional training procedures.

- **Acts a catalyst for feedback.** Oversees the review process to ensure it is conducted properly and in a timely manner. Stays in tune with line officers and supervisors to encourage a free exchange of information. Once the feedback is generated, sees that appropriate information gets to the appropriate administration.

- **Looks for areas of deficiencies.** Identifies components of existing policies that should be revisited, and evaluates areas within the scope of existing policies that could be addressed as stand-alone components.

- **Documents and responds to the feedback.** Captures, catalogs, and responds to feedback from the field. This allows the agency to gauge the effectiveness of a policy over time. What may appear to be insignificant now could become significant at a later date as feedback on additional incidents add to the body of information available. An accurate record of feedback can also serve as evidence if the reasonableness of the agency ever is questioned.

In a small agency, the role of risk manager will likely rest with the chief or sheriff. In large agencies, the responsibility may be assigned to another individual. However, no matter who is given the job, that person needs to have the authority to enforce any action taken by the policy group and to address all disciplinary problems resulting from policy implementation. Perhaps most important, the risk manager needs to be able to intercede wherever necessary to keep the policy process flowing.

Using Feedback

Establishing a process of bringing information on a policy back to you means that you must act on it. You cannot sit on a problem if you know it exists. If a policy is shown to be deficient, it must be changed. If you find your officers are not properly prepared to handle the tasks outlined in the policy, they must be given more training. If you find that some other area of agency operations needs consistent procedures, you need to develop and implement a policy. Failure to do so could expose the agency to a claim of deliberate indifference.

Of course, some feedback may not warrant any action. In that case, you need to document that no action was required and why. As long as you can prove you made your decision in a reasonable manner, you will likely be protected.

In addition, you must close the loop by responding to the person who provided the feedback, and informing him or her of your decision. Officers and supervisors need to know that their comments are not simply disappearing into an administrative black hole. Contact them for clarification or amplification whenever appropriate. As long as they know their input is being considered, they will likely stay engaged in the process.

If you conclude that a report or complaint does not merit action, that does not mean it is not useful. While something may not be a concern right now, it might become one in the future. Feedback gathered today can serve as the basis for further policy development later.

Discussion Questions

1. When it comes to policy, what is meant by closing the loop? Why is it important?

2. Why should the agency assign one person to act as the Policy Risk Manager?

3. Why must you act on policy feedback? Why must that process be documented?

4. Why should you always follow up with personnel offering policy ideas, even if their suggestions are not going to be used?

Eleven

Understanding the
Litigation Process

Objectives

In this chapter, you will learn the following:

- *Understand the importance of documentation*
- *Plan for potential lawsuits*
- *Take additional measures for incidents when litigation is likely*
- *Prepare an adequate defense*
- *Use expert witnesses*
- *Testify*
- *Act on the results of the court case*

Because law enforcement interacts regularly with the public and must constantly balance the demands of society with the Constitutional rights of individuals, incidents inevitably occur where events do not unfold as anticipated. Such incidents may have outcomes ranging from inconsequential to extreme. For law enforcement agencies, it's a matter of "when", not "if" the agency will be involved in a lawsuit.

Being involved in a lawsuit is a troubling and stressful experience because lawsuits are unpredictable and frequently move slowly. A plaintiff can file a suit at almost anytime, from immediately after the incident occurred to whenever the statute of limitations expires, which could be several years. The civil trial can occur months or years after the incident. As time passes, memories fade and must be refreshed regularly to ensure consistency at each phase of the litigation.

The plaintiff's attorneys will investigate everything about the incident. Everyone involved in the incident, as well as the agency itself, will likely be turned inside out. You must prepare for that.

Importance of Accurate Documentation

One of the greatest fallacies in American law enforcement is the belief that the agency is better off not documenting its activities. Many officials are concerned that if something is written down, it will be used against them in a trial or civil case. Consequently, they are reluctant to document incidents when something goes wrong.

However, inaccuracies, omissions, and sloppy reporting provide the plaintiff with ammunition for charging the agency with a cover-up. Even worse, if you routinely avoid documenting incidents, you will not be able to prove that an unfortunate episode is an isolated event. In this situation, the plaintiff could argue that such actions are the custom of the agency, which might result in a significant judgment against the agency.

Developing a standard practice for accurate and complete reporting is one of the most important ways of preparing for potential litigation. Accurate reporting enables you to show that the agency took reasonable steps to mitigate the incident, to investigate the situation, and to demonstrate that the agency acted appropriately regarding policy changes, discipline, and prevention of further incidents. If an incident goes wrong, but your officers took reasonable steps throughout the situation, documentation will help explain the facts.

Planning for a Defense

The defense against any litigation starts with planning. In a general sense, you've already laid the groundwork for a good defense if you have followed the steps outlined in this book.

Initial Steps in Preparing for Litigation

The following points summarize the steps described elsewhere in this book:

- **Develop policies to address areas of high risk to officers and high liability to the agency.** Assess the areas within your jurisdiction that are major areas of concern. As you put policies together to address these areas, consider the needs of the agency, the needs of the officers, and the needs of the community.

- **Institute a process to certify that officers know the policy.** Certify to a policy (and re-certify as necessary) to make sure your personnel know it well. Certification is critical because officers must be able to reconstruct the policy and to explain its operational aspects for the depositions and trial. During litigation, the plaintiff's attorney will dissect the policy, looking for weaknesses. If officers cannot verbalize their understanding of the policy, it could lead to speculation that the officers did not truly understand the policy.

- **Take steps to encourage active supervision.** Provide the resources and support that supervisors need to do their jobs. Line officers need the guidance and perspective that an engaged supervisor provides. Supervisors know their officers best because they are involved in the officer's daily activities and know how much training each officer has had. For this reason, they are often in the best position to make decisions on the most appropriate responses and to evaluate the effectiveness of a policy in action.

- **Use a sound reporting process.** Ensure that officers follow proper procedures when developing their reports, and use the correct forms. It is always advantageous when incident reports follow the policy directives that guided the incident. Officers benefit by having a process for making sure they cover everything, and the agency benefits from the knowledge that all of the relevant facts will be documented consistently.

- **Be able to provide evidence that policy development is an ongoing process.** Maintain an atmosphere of open and honest feedback in which your officers participate readily. Based on officers' recommendations and your own observations, change or amend the policy whenever necessary. Along with any alteration, re-institute the training and enforcement process to ensure that all officers understand the most current version.

- **Consider prioritizing incidents based on outcome.** Use incident reports to identify areas that need attention, and situations that could result in litigation. You can use the debriefing to prioritize the incident, incorporating the priorities into the reporting structure, so that the chain of command can be alerted as needed.

This general plan enables you to respond quickly and efficiently to any problems as they arise.

Additional Measures for High-Risk Incidents

For incidents that will likely result in litigation, such as incidents where injuries or fatalities occurred, or situations that could result in a claim of false arrest or negligence, take the following additional steps to ensure that the agency acts appropriately to preserve evidence. Do not wait until you are notified of legal proceedings.

- **Collect all relevant information.** Implement a retention plan for the documents that need to be saved. It is critical that this be done immediately because items, such as dispatch tapes, are often routinely destroyed or recycled. Destroying any evidence, even inadvertently, gives the appearance that you have something to hide and were trying to cover it up. Save such information as evidence logs, inventory sheets, initial reports, follow-up investigation reports, and any other documentation related to the incident.

- **Communicate with all personnel involved in the incident.** Inform all affected parties that litigation is likely. Too often, officers do not even know the agency is investigating the incident, much less that a lawsuit could be filed. By communicating in the beginning, you enable the officers to better prepare for answering inside queries and for handling the personal stress of pending legal action. Make a list of all personnel who were involved, and keep the list with the other information pertinent to the incident.

- **Reiterate the need for good reporting.** Remind officers that reports must be complete and accurate. Sloppy or incomplete reports are confusing and reflect badly on the officer. Officers should always ask themselves, "Have I included all the necessary statements, facts, and evidence so it is easily understood?" If the report is not clear to the officers, it will not be clear to the jury.

- **Emphasize the gravity of omitting information or altering reports**. Enforce the consequences if someone does alter reports. Officers sometimes do this for fear of incriminating themselves. However, when plaintiffs sue the agency, their attorneys will spend the time and the resources to thoroughly reconstruct the incident. The plaintiff's attorneys will find any witnesses and will uncover any facts that were held back or missed entirely. Omissions, even unintentional ones, destroy an officer's credibility, and cast doubt on every other aspect of the agency's case.

- **Ensure that supervisors also understand the consequences of omissions and alterations.** If a supervisor sees something differently, or has something to add, he or she should write a supplemental report to clarify an officer's account, or have the officer write a supplemental report. *Under no circumstances* should the supervisor tell the officer to change the original report.

- **Consult with legal attorney, risk managers, and insurance carrier.** Inform the people who handle the agency's legal and risk management affairs about the possibility of litigation related to the incident. These professionals might have some additional steps for you to take.

- **Document all of the post-incident preparation for litigation.** Use a standard checklist to ensure that you collect all the information you need, and that you follow a consistent process.(See Figure 21.) Being proactive about collecting and acquiring documentation and information related to an incident demonstrates sound risk management practices, and will only help the defense.

Counseling for Officers

Obviously, the most important consideration is the well-being of the officer. However, it is also critical for a defense effort. Lawsuits are stressful. All members of the agency need to be of sound minds and bodies when going into depositions and trial.

Incidents that result in a high likelihood of litigation, also may indicate that officers need counseling. Stress from such incidents frequently presents some post-incident psychological issues. All officers involved will be affected somehow, even if they do not admit it, or even know it.

Defense Preparation Checkoff Sheet

Incident ID:	Date of incident:

Scene of Incident

☐   All photos and negatives taken (including video tape, if available)

☐   Drawings, sketches, renderings or recreations of scene

☐   List of all those at the scene (including officers, suspects, third parties, witnesses)

☐   Statements from those at the scene

Officers involved in incident

☐   Personnel files

☐   All incident reports

☐   Tapes and transcripts of interviews/debriefings

Suspects involved in incident

☐   Personal information (Any records, history, lien checks, prints, etc.)

☐   Medical reports. if available. (Hospital/Medical Examiner, in case of death)

Third parties involved in incident, if applicable

☐   Personal information (Address, phone, history, etc.)

☐   Medical reports. if available. (Hospital/Medical Examiner, in case of death)

Agency Information

☐   All incident-related reports

☐   Copy of dispatch tapes and official transcript

☐   Investigation notes

☐   Copy of directed patrol policy

☐   Copy of all relevant policies

☐   Copies of all information releases

☐   All relevant correspondences (such as letters to/from attorneys, risk managers, insurance carriers, etc)

Other Pertinent Information

☐   Relevant court records and reports

☐   All newspaper articles

Figure 21: Sample Defense Preparation Checklist

Neglecting the psychological aspects of an incident can cause the officer to have problems later, especially if he or she is asked to relive a traumatic incident during litigation. Many people can block a tragic incident out of their minds until they are put on the spot and have to defend their actions. If the officer has difficulty dealing with the incident, it could damage the defense, even if the officer's actions were appropriate.

Managing a Lawsuit

When you are notified of a lawsuit, first meet with your legal attorney to review the entire case. To properly assess the situation, your attorney needs to know everything about the case, both good and bad. Do not hide anything from your defense attorney. If you hide information from your attorney, he or she will not be able to prepare an adequate defense. Rest assured, lawyers for a plaintiff seeking a multi-million dollar judgment will discover any facts you would rather keep hidden.

The following sections describe the information that your attorney needs in order to effectively review your case.

Incident

Explain what happened in complete detail. Your attorney needs to find out if the steps taken by the officers involved in the case were reasonable and whether the officers, by taking those actions, contributed to the problem. If the agency does a thorough job of handling after-action tasks, this information will be found in the reports, logs, dispatch tapes, and inventory sheets. For this reason, it is important to preserve such items once you learn of an incident that could result in litigation.

Without documentation, the facts are not only subject to interpretation, they are also subject to conjecture. Your attorney will also interview all of the participants to get their accounts of what happened and to understand how certain decisions were made.

Agency

For a general agency perspective, your attorney will want to review a copy of the policy that governed the response being disputed. If the affected policy does not contain a training component, your attorney will also want to see the training policy. This review will include answering questions about the following issues:

- How does the agency train to policy?

- How often is the policy reviewed?

- What mechanism exists for certifying that the officers understand and abide by the policy?

- How does your agency know that the officers take what they learn in training and apply it in actual situations?

While an agency is not constitutionally required to do the last task, having such information can add validity to the claim that the agency places importance on training.

In addition, your attorney will want to review statistical information, such as the number of similar incidents the agency engages in on a weekly or monthly basis and, of those, the number of successful incidents. Be prepared to provide documented evidence to support your statistics. If any previous incidents resulted in lawsuits, provide the information about the cases and their outcomes to your attorney.

Officers Involved

Your attorney will want to review the personnel file of each officer involved in the incident. Some of the following questions may arise for each officer:

- How long has the individual been an officer?

- What training programs has the officer completed?

- When the incident occurred, how long had the officer been on duty?

- Was the officer operating under any agency restrictions?

- In how many similar incidents has that officer been involved? What were the results of those incidents?

- Has the officer been subjected to disciplinary measures in the past? If so, what were the facts and outcomes in each incident?

Follow up

During the meeting with your attorney, you will receive advice on your next steps. Such steps may include the following:

- **Gather in-house information to bolster the case.** Provide any documentation, reports, statistics, or case studies that support your position.

- **Continue the outside investigation of the incident,** such as searching for additional witnesses to confirm your presentation of the facts. Incidents often have numerous witnesses, many of whom may not have been contacted or interviewed during the initial investigation.

- **Arrange private meetings between the attorney and the officers involved.** Ensure that the meetings are conducted in private, without the presence of other line officers, supervisors, administrators, or internal affairs personnel. Officers often give better accounts of what happened when they feel someone is not looking over their shoulder. They need to be able to speak freely about any concerns they might have.

- **Prepare your officers for what is about to transpire.** Have them review their respective areas of involvement, so they can accurately recall the facts associated with the incident.

- **Ensure that the officers involved have a copy of the policy as it existed at the time of the incident.** Too often, especially when a time gap exists between the incident and lawsuit, officers arrive at depositions and cannot even remember what the policy was. This conveys the message that they probably did not understand the policy during the incident, either.

- **Prepare officers for the psychological aspects of the proceedings.** Your officers will be challenged and exposed, both professionally and emotionally. Provide them access to psychological counseling, if necessary. Officers are generally caring human beings, so they will likely show emotion when describing a tragic incident. However, they should also display the confidence that they responded in a reasonable manner.

- **Identify the policy changes that occurred after the incident**. Doing so can work in your favor. As advocated throughout this book, policies should be fluid and dynamic. It is only natural that you would review a policy after a serious incident and adjust it if it's needed. Demonstrating a good understanding of policy and having a well-documented process by which those changes were made supports the fact that yours is a proactive agency that acts in a responsible manner. Of course, you should seek advice from your legal attorney before making any significant alterations. Changes can be made, but they must be made in a manner that supports your case, not hinders it.

Using Expert Witnesses

If your agency is being sued for a constitutional violation of an individual's rights, consider engaging an expert witness on your agency's behalf. An expert is a person who, based on education, training and experience, is able to provide information about a specific aspect of a case to a jury. Expert witnesses use their knowledge and expertise to explain particular facts about the incident. Typically, the information provided by the expert witness falls outside jury's area of knowledge.

To be an expert, a person must be qualified by knowledge, skill, experience, training, or education. The best experts are those who have held and still hold policy-making positions, who have a blend of academic and practical experience, and who are not in it for the money.

Base the number of experts involved in a case on the number of issues raised. For instance, a case resulting from the scenario posed in Appendix B involves issues of pursuit; detention center procedures for screening, restraining and obtaining medical attention for suspects; and the administration of medical attention. In that scenario, you might have three different experts testifying, one for each issue. Each case is different, so the number of experts needed varies.

Getting an Expert Involved

Experts should get involved as soon as a suit is filed. Involving experts early enables you and your attorney to benefit from their specialized knowledge, and will affect how the case is handled. The expert's opinion can help determine the degree of exposure the agency faces. If it becomes apparent that the officers or the agency were in the wrong, you want to find that out as early as possible so that you can take steps to minimize the damage.

In addition, having experts involved early may enable you to defuse negative public opinion and to counter the assertions made by the plaintiff's attorney. Almost every big case these days is tried in the press as well as in court. The community in general will likely draw some conclusion about the case, which may or may not be favorable. The plaintiff's attorneys and their experts will most likely be making statements to bolster their position in the eyes of the public.

Selecting an Expert

There are a few things to keep in mind when considering who should be the expert representing your side of a case. First, an expert must have the education, training, and experience to provide a substantive opinion on the issue in question, and he or she must be able to convey that opinion so that the jury can understand the issue. Consider the implications of a case where a suspect dies while in police custody. Most people on a jury do not understand how a relatively healthy person can die while being restrained after an altercation with police. The jurors may assume that the police must have done something to harm the suspect, which is not always the case. If your officers followed proper procedures, your expert must be able to address the issue of sudden death syndrome in a substantive, yet clear manner.

Next, consider if you want a person from outside the agency to serve as your expert. In larger agencies, skilled people may exist in-house who can address the liability issues presented. However, the plaintiff's attorney will question your expert's objectivity. An inside expert's opinion is influenced by the fact that he or she is employed by the agency being accused of wrongdoing. You also open the door to a claim that you had to stay within the agency because anyone looking at the case objectively would not take your side. On the plus side, using an inside expert shows the jury that your people are competent, and that you are not afraid to thoroughly examine the agency's response to the incident.

Selecting an outside expert has its own problems. The jury will ask what the expert has to gain by presenting their testimony. In many cases, it is money. Many experts base their opinions on who is paying them. For a fee, these experts selectively apply their expertise to render a conclusion that meets with the approval of whomever employs them.

Don't kid yourself, the money is on the other side. Many people, including ex-law enforcement officers, would love to charge for their opinions. However, the mere status of being an ex-peace officer does not qualify a person to be an expert witness. Use your own knowledge of who the experts are and provide this information to your attorney.

Working with Experts

Be very careful in how your work with your experts. Generally, it is best to simply meet with your experts and discuss your case with them. It is very rare for an expert to generate a written report. Given the rules of discovery, if something is written down, you may have to furnish a copy of that material to the plaintiff.

More and more, federal courts are going from a process of discovery to a process of disclosure. The courts are saying that the other side has a right to know what you are doing. However, you do still have a right to prepare your case in confidence. Therefore, even though attorneys for the other side may have a right to know that you have retained an expert, they do not have a right to know what the expert is telling you, as long as that expert is not going to testify on your behalf.

The notion of protecting an expert from discovery goes a step further if the expert is an individual from inside the agency. Since the agency is the client, anything that an employee of the agency tells your attorney is protected by the attorney/client privilege. As long as an inside expert does not testify, the information that they provide is strictly non-discoverable.

However, if an inside expert is going to testify, part of the attorney/client privilege will be waived. Therefore, some of the information provided by the inside expert is subject to discovery, and the plaintiff's attorney likely has the right to question your expert in a deposition.

Testifying

Litigation often progresses slowly. It can take several years to complete the process, from the initial incident through the trial. All officers need to refresh their memories regularly because statements made in one phase of a lawsuit can easily cause problems later, if you are not prepared or careful.

Depositions

Depositions are part of the discovery process, with attorneys for both sides asking questions of various people about specific issues pertaining to the case. You cannot win or lose your case at this stage, but the strength of your case is made known during the deposition. Since the strength of that position often leads to a settlement before trial, the importance of the deposition cannot be overemphasized.

Never walk into a deposition without preparing for it. Attorneys representing the agency will likely work with you so that you will know what to expect, but you should take some additional steps on your own.

- **Know the policy in question.** Line officers, supervisors, and others directly involved must know the guidelines set by the policy that directed the incident. Administrators may not need to know the policy in minute detail, but they are required to show that a reasonable policy exists, and that it was developed and implemented in a logical manner.

- **Know the facts of the case.** Everyone involved must know exactly what happened in the incident and be able to articulate those facts clearly and concisely.

- **Read the reports.** This is especially important for line officers. Police reports are frequently terse, and can easily be misinterpreted. Officers must be able to explain their reports and to expand on the report where necessary.

In addition to the above steps, expert witnesses need to avoid some common mistakes:

- **Don't fake your way through a response.** Admit it if you don't know the answer. To do otherwise risks destroying credibility and the beneficial parts of the testimony.

- **Don't avoid a challenge to your objectivity.** Be prepared to address the issue of why you are testifying. The opposing attorney will likely challenge your objectivity by asking about how many times you have testified on behalf of the agency and how much compensation you receive. Answer such questions matter-of-factly.

Opposing attorneys are looking for weaknesses, areas that they can exploit at trial. They may request that video cameras be used to record the depositions. Videotapes do give accurate records, but they also provide the opportunity to study your voice inflection and body language in response to certain questions. Opposing attorneys search these for "hot buttons" that can be pushed later.

All officers must behave professionally at all times. Your attorney will attempt to keep the questioning from getting sidetracked onto spurious issues, but each officer's deportment should reflect positively on the agency. Everyone should appear interested in the proceedings; no one should give the impression of being bored or disgusted. While a case cannot be lost in a deposition, a disrespectful attitude or a wayward comment can do significant damage to the case.

Courtroom and Trial

While a deposition is used to gather information, the trial is where the case is built for jury consideration. Prepare for a trial in much the same way as you would for a deposition: review the policy involved, the facts of the case, and all reports pertaining to the incident. Also, review your deposition. In many instances, courtroom testimony simply rehashes the depositions, only this time for the jury.

Appearance and deportment are crucial. First impressions have a lasting impact. The judge and jury will hear conflicting facts in case. You want them to believe your version. Project a professional demeanor:

- Be on time when you are scheduled to appear and notify your attorney that you have arrived.

- Maintain confidentiality by never discussing the case with other witnesses or the media.

- Dress appropriately, wearing your uniform or a suit.

- Observe the formalities of the courtroom. Even when you are not testifying, you will be noticed.

- Address the judge with respect. Always stand when he or she enters or leaves.

- Stay alert and appear interested in the case. Do not show disrespect, disgust, or boredom at any time.

- Walk normally to take the witness stand. Remember, you will always be under inspection.

You have one possible advantage in that juries tend to identify with witnesses. Courtrooms are the domain of judges and lawyers. Jurors tend to relate to the witnesses because they have been brought to court, just as the jury has been. If you act arrogantly or do not take the proceedings seriously, the members of the jury are less likely to view you favorably, which will negatively affect your testimony.

Guidelines for Answering Questions

For direct examination, your attorney will probably lead you through a series of questions similar to those asked during deposition. Under cross examination, the opposing attorney will try to show that your actions were contrary to what was required by policy. When it comes to responding to such questions, use the guidelines described in the following sections.

- **Tell the truth.** This is by far the most important rule. Answer all questions truthfully and to the best of your knowledge. You are under oath. Nothing is worth perjuring yourself. Once you do that, you have destroyed what you stand for.

- **Be consistent.** Keep in mind that, through your deposition, you have already testified under oath. If what you say in court is not consistent with what you said in the deposition, your credibility will be called into question. You may be able to expand on a previous response to clear up any discrepancies or ambiguities, but the crux of your testimony needs to be the same.

- **Talk in a normal voice and use proper language.** Avoid jargon and never act glib or flippant. To make your point, your answers must be easy to understand and sincere. Also, try not to speak too fast. This helps both the jurors and the court reporter, who must capture everything you say for the record.

- **Be concise.** Speak only about matters of fact; do not exaggerate or speculate. Provide observations, not opinions. Only expert witnesses should render opinions.

- **Listen carefully to the questions.** What you testify to is what you will be held to, so make sure you understand the question. If you do not understand a question, ask the attorney to repeat or clarify it. Also, never anticipate a question by answering it before it is asked.

- **Know the facts, but don't memorize the answers.** Be prepared, but not too rehearsed. You don't want to appear like a machine that memorized a script. Give some thought to each question before responding.

- **Don't pretend you know something you don't.** You don't always have to have an answer. Instead, say you don't recall or you don't have that information. Time erodes memory; people understand that.

- **Anticipate possible objections.** Discuss this with your attorney beforehand. When you are asked a question that may be objected to, don't blurt out an answer. Give your attorney time to object and the judge time to rule.

- **Control your emotions.** This can be difficult. When attorneys for the plaintiff know you have damaging facts regarding their case, they will attack your credibility. Tactics you may encounter include getting you angry, personalizing the incident, attempting to confuse you and sidetracking to unrelated issues to catch you off guard. If they can demonstrate that you are less than what you appear to be, or get you to fly off the handle, your testimony will be devalued. On the other hand, if you stay calm and courteous at all times, you will come across as someone who is knowledgeable, thoughtful, and confident in the information you are presenting. and if the opposing attorney continues a barrage of attacks, it will turn off the judge and jury. Even if you get tripped up, you will likely be viewed sympathetically. So stay in control, communicate clearly, and show respect to all parties.

After the Testimony

After finishing your testimony, critique your performance. How effective was your preparation? Did you express the points you wanted to make in the manner you wanted to make them? Were you able to present and support evidence and legal technicalities relevant to this particular case? Did the jury seem to understand your responses?

Ask your attorney to give you a fair assessment of your testimony. Were you a strong witness for your case? How could you have been stronger? How well did you hold up under cross-examination?

The purpose of this exercise is to start preparing you for the next case. Your involvement with this case may be over, but you may need to testify again for some other case. Analyzing your performance will help make you a better witness in the future, and a stronger advocate for both the agency and yourself. This, in turn, contributes to the total risk management process, which leads to policies that are truly defensible, the same process that has been advocated throughout this book.

Acting on the Results of the Case

The outcome of the case determines your course of action. If an out-of-court settlement was reached, inform all the parties involved of the details, including the reasons for the decision. Many officers take lawsuits personally, and want to fight regardless of the situation. However, a settlement is not always an admission of wrongdoing. You might choose a settlement for the following reasons:

- The case had a poor chance of prevailing in court.

- It might have been more cost effective to settle the case rather than participating in a long, drawn-out proceeding.

If you lose the case after a trial, examine your policies and practices to make the necessary changes. In this situation, you may find that what you considered as reasonable is not, according to the courts. Make the changes so that your officers have the tools they need to do their jobs in a safe, efficient manner that is in line with the public's interests.

Most important, learn from mistakes but don't overreact. Do not adopt the attitude that "We did everything we were supposed to do and still lost, so we'll simply do nothing next time." Some agencies have taken this position when it comes to pursuits. After losing a court case, they have decided they will no longer conduct pursuits, regardless of the situation. This is a self-defeating attitude that does not serve the community.

It is true that you can do everything according to the book and still have a judgment found against you. Do not give up. Avoid the second-guessing that so often accompanies a negative judgment. Instead, use the experience to create change, if change is necessary, and to reassure your officers. Emphasize the fact that the agency and officers worked together and will continue to do so in the future. Tell them that the policy will be reviewed and changed where needed. State that, with their input, you will give them a policy that will be able to stand scrutiny the next time a case such as this one comes up. Above all else, stress that the first priority of the agency will always be to develop policies that enable officers to perform their duties safely and efficiently. Officers must know that their safety and the public's safety will never be compromised.

Discussion Questions

1. Why are so many law enforcement administrators reluctant to document incidents? Why is this the wrong course of action?

2. What steps should be taken when an incident occurs that will likely lead to a lawsuit?

3. Why should psychological counseling be a crucial part of any litigation defense?

4. What steps should you take when you are notified that a lawsuit has been filed against the agency?

5. What types of information will your attorney want to have in order to plan for a defense?

6. Why should all the officers involved be kept informed throughout the process of litigation?

7. What is an expert witness?

8. What are the advantages and disadvantages of using expert witnesses?

9. What do you need to do to prepare for a deposition?

10. What are the keys to providing effective testimony?

11. What lessons should be taken from a lawsuit?

Notes

Sample Policy

This book contains sample polices provided by the Michigan Municipal League. Chapter 5 incorporates examples from the *Use of Force* policy. This appendix provides a description of a policy process and a sample policy for *Post-Force Reporting*.

These policies were developed through the Law Enforcement Action Forum (LEAF). This organization provides opportunities for Michigan law enforcement agencies to meet, to exchange ideas, and to address new problems confronting agencies statewide. LEAF works with risk management groups to create policies that address such issues.

The purpose of LEAF is to reduce the risks facing law enforcement agencies by creating policies that both protect officers from harm and protect the agency from legal claims.

If your state does not have such an organization, create one. Contact the following people:

- State representatives who are on committees that deal with law enforcement issues

- Risk management agencies

- Other state organizations that meet and deal with law enforcement issues

The Liability and Property Pool of the Michigan Municipal League has assisted others in creating such organizations. If you would like assistance, you can contact the pool at www.mmlpool.org.

LEAF Process

The initial purpose of Michigan's Law Enforcement Action Forum (LEAF) was modest compared to its current role in Michigan law enforcement. In 1992, police liability claims were a growing concern among insurers for Michigan's cities, villages, and townships. Loss control professionals for the Michigan Municipal League's Liability and Property Pool suggested that it might be more effective for police chiefs to develop their own loss control standards, rather than have an insurer impose loss control recommendations without police department input.

LEAF has, for the past 11 years, combined the creative energy of brainstorming with the due diligence of professional, legal, and scholarly review, to create a system of policy development that is a model worth imitating.

First, bring together a workable number of Police Chiefs, Public Safety Directors, and Sheriffs. We recommend more than four, but no more than 10 participants. Second, designate or appoint a meeting facilitator - someone to develop and distribute an agenda and information before the meeting, someone to keep the meeting on task and to end the meeting on time. Third, add an attorney whose specialty is municipal and police liability, and you have the groundwork for success.

The law enforcement professionals comprising your group must be committed to this process. LEAF is more akin to compounding interest than to a slot machine jackpot. The most impressive results will occur over a period of years, not after a few meetings.

A strong facilitator is a must. There aren't any shrinking violets in the police chief ranks. Strong personalities are necessary for successful policy development, and a strong facilitator needs to direct the group's efforts and to help them stay on task.

It helps greatly to have a legal advisor who has experience in all aspects of municipal and police liability, including as defense counsel during trial. The eloquence of the policy is less important than how the policy will be perceived by potential litigants, judges, and juries. Involving competent legal counsel during policy development adds legitimacy to the process.

Policy development is only part of the story. Once the policy is developed, it is not allowed to rest. LEAF continuously reviews and, where necessary, revises its policies to recognize changes in the legal and professional environment in which Michigan's police officers operate. Member agencies receive revised policies promptly, with adequate explanation and instruction for effective implementation.

The *LEAF Manual for Law Enforcement Risk Control* is on the World Wide Web and available for members of the Michigan Municipal League's Insurance Programs. The web site makes the delivery of the polices, the related review of law, and topical support materials even more convenient for the members to stay up to date. The web site is updated regularly with new or updated materials that LEAF has developed.

We are pleased to offer the following policy as a representative sample of the results of LEAF's efforts.

Sample Policy and Procedures for Post-Force Reporting Process

I. PURPOSE

To establish a reporting and review mechanism that shall be applied when officers use compliance controls, physical controls, or a weapon to overcome resistive behavior, and use of force incidents that result in injury or death.

II. DEFINITIONS

A. *"Active Resistance"* is defined as that resistance demonstrated by a subject(s) who physically resists or threatens to physically resist by assuming an aggressive posture, and who does not comply with verbal direction. Other examples of active resistance include, but are not necessarily limited to, a subject's attempt to defeat an officer's attempt to establish control by pulling away, turning away or pushing away from the officer without demonstrating an intent to injure or harm the officer.

B. *"Control"* is the method/methods an officer uses to neutralize the unlawful actions of a subject, or to protect the subject from injuring himself or others.

C. *"Compliance Control"* is the use of soft empty hand techniques (e.g., joint locks, pressure points, etc.) or authorized control devices (e.g., baton, etc., when used as a compliance control device) to control resistance and gain compliance with verbal commands or directions. Compliance controls are used to gain compliance and to control low levels of subject resistance where the subject has not demonstrated an intent to injure or harm the officer.

D. *"Force"* is the attempt to establish control through physical means, in the presence of resistance. All force is a means of control; however, control can at times be achieved without the use of physical force.

E. *"Resistance"* is defined as the subject's attempt to evade an officer's attempts to establish control.

III. SUBJECT RESISTANCE/OFFICER CONTROL REPORTING REQUIREMENTS:

A. Applications of officer control, while either on or off duty, that result in injury, complaints of injury, or that involve the use of a weapon or compliance controls (ADD K-9 if applicable); of any type, shall be reported by the involved officer(s) to the on-duty commander/ supervisor, or the senior officer or on-call supervisor in the absence of an on-duty commander/supervisor, as soon as practical.

B. All incidents involving subject resistance at or above the level of active resistance shall be reported in detail by the involved officer(s).

C. Before the completion of the officer's tour of duty, he shall complete an incident report and the departmental Subject Resistance/Officer Control report.

D. The commander/supervisor will review incidents in which an officer uses force to control subject resistance.

E. After conducting a review of the circumstances attending the use of force, the commander/supervisor shall submit a written report to the (Chief, Director, Sheriff) through proper channels.

IV. PROCEDURE TO BE FOLLOWED WHEN FIREARM IS DISCHARGED

A. Notification and report are required by officer(s) involved whenever an officer discharges a firearm, outside of training or recreational use.

B. The officer shall verbally notify the on-duty supervisor or on-call supervisor as soon as time and circumstances permit.

C. The officer who discharged a firearm shall file a written report of the incident through established channels with the department and a copy with the officer(s) supervisor by the end of their tour of duty, or as soon as reasonably possible, if mitigating conditions exist.

D. If the officer who discharged a firearm is hospitalized or fatally injured in their tour of duty and incapable of filing the report as required above, the supervisor is responsible for filing as complete a report as possible pending further departmental investigation.

V. DEATH OR INJURY OF A PERSON

A. In the event that a person is killed or seriously injured as a result of an officer's activity;

1. Said officer(s) shall be relieved of duty by the (CHIEF, SHERIFF, DIRECTOR or his designee), and placed on Administrative Leave. The department's response should be as outlined in the Critical Incident Management policy, located elsewhere in this manual.

2. While on Administrative Leave officers shall remain available and in communication with the (Chief, Director, Sheriff) or his designee.

3. The (Chief, Director, Sheriff) may reinstate the officer to administrative duty during the investigation of the incident, or

4. The (Chief, Director, Sheriff) may fully reinstate the officer at such time that the Chief of Police determines that the officer was acting in a reasonable and responsible manner based upon the circumstances of the incident.

B. The officer(s) shall turn over the weapon used, if any, in the incident to the first or nearest available supervisor. (Editor's Comment: Departments may consider providing a substitute weapon to the officer.)

C. The officer(s) shall provide reports of the incident.

D. The (Chief, Director, Sheriff) shall be notified of the incident by the supervisor in charge, as soon as practical.

E. Such incidents shall be investigated by persons designated by the department. Said investigator(s) may request the assistance of the Prosecutor's Office and/or any law enforcement agency having jurisdiction.

VI. INCIDENT REVIEW

A. An incident review will be conducted as soon as reasonably possible after an officer uses force.

B. The review should consist of an examination of the circumstances surrounding the incident. Of particular note in the review should be the appropriateness of the use of force based on all applicable laws and departmental guidelines, policies and training practices.

C. The review shall be for the purpose of fact finding only, and is not intended to become a disciplinary element of the investigative process.

D. Annually, the (Chief, Director or Sheriff), or his designee shall conduct a documented analysis of the previous year use of force incidents.

VII. COMPLIANCE

Violations of this policy, or portions thereof, may result in disciplinary action.

VIII. OFFICERS ASSIGNED TO OTHER AGENCIES

Officers of this department assigned to or assisting other law enforcement agencies will be guided by this policy.

IX. APPLICATION

This order constitutes department policy, and is not intended to enlarge the employer's or employee's civil or criminal liability in any way. It shall not be construed as the creation of a higher legal standard of safety or care in an evidentiary sense with respect to third party claims insofar as the employer's or employee's legal duty as imposed by law.

Policy History:
Accepted   October 5, 1993
Reviewed November 11, 1993
Amended October 6, 1994
Amended October 25, 1995
Reviewed October 15, 1996

Reviewed October 14, 1997
Amended September 30, 1998
Reviewed September 30, 1999
Reviewed September 28, 2000
Amended September 28, 2000
Amended September26, 2001
Amended September 26, 2002
Amended September 25, 2003

CALEA: 1.3.6
       1.3.7
       1.3.8
       1.3.13

ADDITIONAL POLICY SECTIONS

When implementing a departmental policy on the reporting of the use of force, administrators should consider adoption of additional policy elements that may be unique to the operation of their department. While some issues are not addressed in the enclosed policy document, departments whose operations involve these activities should incorporate policy language, which will provide specific guidance in these areas. Desirable policy addenda are outlined here. (Passages appearing in brackets [ ] are advisory in nature, and are not intended to be used as policy language.)

This section should be utilized to assist a department in establishing an Incident Review Committee:

[It should be inserted into the *"Sample Policy and Procedures for Post Force Reporting Process"*, with appropriate modifications made to the remainder of the policy to reflect the change.]

Incident Review Committee

a. There is established an Incident Review Committee consisting of the following members, along with others who may be designated by the Chief of Police:

1. the Training Officer of the department;
2. the division commander of the officer(s) involved;
3. the supervisor of the officer(s) involved.

b. The Chief of Police shall designate the Committee Chair. The Committee Chair shall call a meeting of the Committee within a reasonable time after the Chief of Police brings the report of the incident to their attention.

c. The Committee is authorized to review the circumstances surrounding the incident and to make recommendations for improvements in training, policy or other operational areas relevant to their findings.

d. The Committee shall serve as a fact-finding body only, and will not become a disciplinary arm of the investigative process.

Appendix B

Case Study

The following case study demonstrates a practical application of policy issues in everyday circumstances. The facts of the case are based on the truth, but are a compilation of two incidents that took place.

Case Facts

On the evening of June 16, Hugo Burned picked up his friend, Mike Feat, to drink beer and to go cruising in Hugo's father's full-size black Blazer. They lived in a small community just north of Lug City, a major metropolitan area in a Midwestern state. Hugo was 20; Mike was 19. Hugo had used a false ID to purchase a six-pack of beer.

When Hugo picked Mike up, Mike already seemed intoxicated. Unknown to Hugo, Mike had consumed about 3/4 gallon of windshield wiper solvent. Mike knew windshield wiper solvent contained methyl alcohol rather than ethyl alcohol, but he simply thought the substance would give him a quick buzz.

The two consumed beer until around midnight. Then, they went to a local supermarket and began stealing shopping carts. Hugo drove down the road while Mike held onto the shopping carts from the back of the Blazer, and then let them go to see how far the carts would roll.

The store manager reported the theft of the carts to the state police dispatching agency. The state police broadcasted the theft over their central dispatch, which reached the police agencies in Lug City, the suburb where the store was located, and the county sheriff's department.

Deputy Van was on routine patrol just after midnight at the edge of town. He was on a four-lane, divided highway traveling south when he noticed a black Blazer traveling north. As soon as he spotted the Blazer, the vehicle accelerated to a high rate of speed.

Deputy Van continued south to a turnaround, crossed over to head north and accelerated to make a traffic stop on the Blazer. As he proceeded north, he realized the situation had changed dramatically and dangerously because the suspect vehicle was still speeding excessively, but now had its lights off. Deputy Van activated his overhead lights, but not his siren. He thought the siren would not be effective since the Blazer was between 0.25 and 0.5 miles ahead of him and accelerating.

Deputy Van followed the vehicle and realized it was increasing its distance from his vehicle. He saw the brake lights go on, then saw the vehicle turn to the right, down a two-lane, asphalt, country road. At this point, Deputy Van knew he would not catch the other vehicle, but he also knew that the road would be extremely dangerous for anyone traveling without lights on, and that such a vehicle would be an extreme danger to anyone else coming from the opposite direction. Because the country road was hilly, Deputy Van felt that the operator of the other vehicle would crash, more likely sooner than later, so he continued to follow the vehicle and left his overhead lights on.

The country road ended in T-intersection 3 miles from where the Blazer turned onto it. At end of this T-intersection, Deputy Van found the vehicle about 150 feet off the road where it had struck two trees. Later investigation showed the deputy was 0.7 miles behind the Blazer when the crash occurred.

Deputy Van went to investigate. He found Mike walking around at the scene. He appeared to be intoxicated, but otherwise uninjured. Hugo, however, was critically injured. Deputy Van radioed for help, and then asked Mike what he had been drinking. Mike was swearing at the officer and was uncooperative, but did say he had consumed methyl alcohol. Deputy Van did not know what this meant.

Paramedics and two ambulances arrived. One ambulance took Hugo away. A paramedic who was also a deputy sheriff attempted to examine Mike, but Mike would not cooperate. He did not appear to have any injuries; he simply appeared to be highly intoxicated. His name was run through the lien machine; it turned out there were outstanding warrants for his arrest in Lug City. He was told to get into the ambulance to be taken to the hospital. He was also told that, after being examined, he would be turned over to officers in Lug City.

Mike refused to go in the ambulance and continued to be obnoxious. Therefore, the deputy/paramedic called the hospital and talked to the doctor on staff in the emergency room, telling him that he had a highly intoxicated person who had been involved in a serious auto accident but did not appear to have any serious injuries. The doctor said that it was important to watch Mike, but gave no other instructions. Deputy Van did not relay the information that Mike had been consuming methyl alcohol earlier.

Because Mike was highly intoxicated and extremely obnoxious, Deputy Van decided to transfer Mike to Lug City. Lug City was contacted and advised there would be a prisoner pick-up at a water tower. No further information was given to Lug City. Deputy Van delivered the prisoner to Officer Harvey from Lug City at the appointed location. At this time, Mike was complaining of severe stomach pain.

Lug City had a policy of not accepting prisoners who are sick or incapacitated. This fact was well known to Deputy Van. Officer Harvey expressed some concerns about accepting Mike as a prisoner. Deputy Van replied, "I thought I was going to have to spend a couple of hours with him at the hospital, but they told me just to watch him closely for a while because he's intoxicated."

Officer Harvey assumed Mike had been to the hospital, seen by a doctor, and cleared medically. He noted that Mike was holding his stomach, wobbly on his feet, and slurring his words. However, Officer Harvey perceived Mike as simply appearing to be highly intoxicated since he was acting in a manner consistent with someone in that state. Mike was verbally abusive, but otherwise not uncooperative. He was handcuffed, according to procedure, and taken to the Lug City Police Department, where he was booked.

Mike, obviously drunk, continued to be obnoxious and to have mood swings, which Officer Harvey believed was typical behavior for someone under the influence of alcohol. The breathalyzer was administered twice. The first time, it registered 0.17. It was believed to be a false reading because of Mike's lack of cooperation. A second breathalyzer was performed, and showed that Mike had a blood alcohol level of 0.24. The breathalyzer was taken, not to obtain criminal charges, but to give the detention officers information about Mike's blood level in case he wanted to bond out. At a 0.24, the officers knew it would take approximately 12 hours before his blood level would be within the legal limit.

Throughout the booking, Mike's conduct was typical of an intoxicated person. Occasionally, he responded to questions; other times he did not. He had a tendency to wander off, even while other people were talking to him.

While Officer Harvey was removing the laces from his shoes, Mike told him, "I drank methyl alcohol."

Officer Harvey did not know what methyl alcohol was, but he thought it was probably something bad. He looked back at Mike and said, "If you had done that, don't you think you would have died by now."

Mike said, "Yeah, probably." Nothing further was said about what he had drunk.

Mike continued to be verbally offensive. Because of this, the detention officer decided to leave his handcuffs on and to put him in a solitary cell, not in with the general prison population. This was a cell where he could be watched. Officer Harvey had no further contact with Mike.

Mike remained in the detoxification cell until the shift change three hours later. The new sergeant coming on duty and the detention officer checked him. Mike was found on a bunk, lying on his side with the cuffs still in place. The records of his booking were reviewed and showed he was in cuffs because he had become combative. The cuffs were then checked to make sure they were not too tight. The officer continued to make periodic observations of him, although no officer actually went

Defensible Policies

into the cell, checked his pulse, or looked at him closely until another three hours had passed.

At that time, the detention officer observed that Mike was lying on his back with his handcuffs still behind him, and had mucus or discharge near his nose or mouth. The detention officer was concerned and reported it to his sergeant. The two of them went back to the cell and rolled Mike over. As they turned him over, Mike fell from the bunk and struck his forehead on the floor, causing a cut just above his left eyebrow.

The detention officer noticed that the cut was very small and did not bleed much, even though it was a cut to the head. He reported to his sergeant that there was a cut. The sergeant, who was standing at the doorway as required by policy, did not observe the cut, but both the sergeant and the detention officer had heard Mike make a noise when he was rolled over. The sound was consistent with what one would hear from a person who being aroused from a deep sleep. The officer removed the handcuffs and continued to check Mike periodically.

Two hours later, the detention officer noticed that Mike was not breathing. He immediately called for help and started CPR. Mike was rushed to the hospital, where he could not be revived.

The preliminary autopsy reported that Mike died of choking. However, blood tests later revealed that he died because of massive methyl alcohol poisoning. The autopsy revealed that the cut to the head was, in fact, very deep and should have bled profusely. Because of this, the medical examiner came to the conclusion that Mike was already dead when he was rolled over and bumped his head. The sigh that the officers heard was air escaping from the body when it was moved.

Policy Issues

1. Deputy Van knew from the dispatch that people in a black Blazer had been stealing shopping carts. Since this is a juvenile act, should he have recognized that the operator of

the Blazer was a young person and should this have affected his decision as to whether to make a traffic stop?

2. The operator of the Blazer did not turn out his lights until the officer began pursuit. Since this hazardous action appeared to have been a direct result of Deputy Van's decision to make the traffic stop, should the officer have immediately discontinued his efforts at making a traffic stop?

3. By the time the Blazer pulled onto the two-lane, country road, it should have been apparent to the officer that the driver was not going to stop. Did Deputy Van's continued use of his overhead lights, which could be observed by the driver of the Blazer who was some distance ahead, directly contribute to the accident?

4. Can a claim for a constitutional violation based on the Fourteenth Amendment's due process concept or the Fourth Amendment's reasonable search and seizure concept be made under these circumstances?

5. Does the crashing Blazer constitute a seizure under the Fourth Amendment, given that the crash occurred while the law enforcement officer was 0.7 miles away?

6. Did Deputy Van's failure to inform anyone at the scene that Mike had said he had consumed methyl alcohol constitute a deliberate indifference to a serious medical need?

7. Was the decision not to transport Mike to the hospital by ambulance a deliberate indifference to a serious medical need?

8. Did Deputy Van deliberately lead Officer Harvey into believing Mike had been to the hospital, and does this give rise to a constitutional claim?

9. Were the detention-screening procedures by the Lug City Police Department adequate?

10. Did the comment by Mike to Officer Harvey that he had consumed methyl alcohol put Officer Harvey on notice that a serious medical condition existed? Was Officer Harvey deliberately indifferent to this condition?

11. Although periodic checks were made of Mike, does the fact that these were only visual checks give rise to a claim of deliberate indifference to a serious medical need?

12. When Mike cut his head but did not come to, did the officers have actual knowledge that Mike was in extreme distress and should medical help have been summoned at that time?

13. Should the officers have tried to rouse Mike out of his apparent stupor when he banged his head and did not come to?

14. Should a call for medical help have been made because of the cut head, even though the cut was determined at the scene to be very minor?

15. If jail policy procedures required that a person who becomes incapacitated in the jail be taken to the hospital, were those procedures violated when it was determined during the various visual checks that Mike was unconscious, even though he was thought to be sleeping off a drunk?

16. Does the concept of deliberate indifference to a serious medical need require more than just casual observation of an unconscious person in a cell, even though there is a known probable reason for this state of unconsciousness (in this instance, intoxication with the blood level of 0.24)?

Notes

Impact of HIPAA on Law Enforcement

$\mathbf{D}$epending on your perspective, HIPAA (Health Insurance Portability and Accountability Act of 1996) is either the best thing since peppermint candy or the perfect example of how even the best intentions can go awry.

Purpose

HIPAA was created in the 1990s to address to specific problems:

- **Lack of health insurance:** The United States does not have universal health insurance. Consequently, people who had health insurance through their jobs would lose that insurance if they left their jobs for any reason. HIPAA legislation enabled people who had health insurance through their jobs to take the insurance with them when they left. Anyone who has lost health insurance and then needed serious medical treatment knows the value of the portability aspect of HIPAA.

- **Invasion of patient privacy when insurance companies sold information:** In the 1990s, some insurance companies were selling information on patients to other insurance companies, to prospective employers, and other entities who wanted to use this information. These sales occurred without the knowledge or permission of the affected patients, and information was frequently misinterpreted by the recipient of the information. Once these practices were exposed, Congress decided to do something about it. The result was the accountability portion of the act, and it is this part of HIPAA that most impacts law enforcement.

Issues for Law Enforcement

Part of the HIPAA legislation included a fine of up to $50,000, which could be levied against any medical provider who created a medical record and improperly (maybe even inadvertently) disclosed it to an outside entity. The obligation to protect the patient's privacy is directed to the entity that creates the record.

Because of this obligation and the stiff penalties involved, medical service providers who generate a record of service now do not want to share information pertaining to that service with anyone. This reluctance makes certain aspects of law enforcement, such as charging a person who has injured another with the specific crime based on the extent of injuries, almost impossible.

What medical personnel may not understand is that the legislation contains exceptions that allow law enforcement personnel to obtain medical information relating to their lawful duties, under any one of the following circumstances:

- The protected party is a victim of a crime (including abuse, neglect, or domestic violence) and disclosure is necessary to prevent serious harm to the individual or other potential victims. OR, the victim cannot provide the information to law enforcement due to incapacitation or emergency, and an immediate enforcement activity that depends on the disclosure would be materially and adversely affected by waiting until the victim is able to agree to the disclosure. State statutes can require individuals in certain professions to report suspected child abuse or neglect.

- The disclosure provides limited information related to reporting a crime in emergencies if the disclosure appears necessary to alert law enforcement to the commission and nature of a crime, the location of a crime or of the victim(s) of the crime, as well as the identity, description, and location of the perpetrator (including a fugitive, material witness, or missing person).

- For victims of a crime, law enforcement may obtain the information if it is needed to determine if a law has been violated by someone other than the victim, and the information is not intended to be used against the victim.

- If the medical provider believes in good faith that such disclosure is necessary to prevent or lessen a serious and imminent threat to the health or safety of an individual or the public, and providing such information can reasonably prevent or lessen the threat (including protecting the target of the threat), or is necessary for law enforcement to identify and/or apprehend an individual.

- The covered entity may release health information about a deceased individual to law enforcement if the entity suspects that such a death may have resulted from criminal conduct.

Despite these clear exceptions, numerous situations have occurred where medical providers have refused to provide information to law enforcement. For example, an EMT at an accident scene refuses to tell an investigating police officer the extent of the victim's injuries. This caution is clearly unwarranted, and is covered by the HIPAA exception that allows the provider to give this information when the matter is under investigation.

In addition, if the EMT provides the information to the police officer at the scene, it is not revealing medical information within the meaning of HIPAA. Police officers need to know the extent and type of injuries so that they can properly charge the perpetrator. In such cases, the difference between a misdemeanor and a felony hinges on the extent of a victim's injuries.

In cases of child and spousal abuse, most states mandate that physicians report the victim's medical condition. It is a crime to knowingly withhold this information. Physicians and other medical providers may believe that they are being pulled in different directions by what they view as competing policies. In fact, these policies are not in conflict and the medical community needs to be assured of this.

Working with the Medical Community

To allay the medical community's fears and to ensure that police officers receive the information they need to do their jobs, law enforcement and the medical community must work together to build a process.

The respective risk managers at the local hospitals and within the law enforcement agencies, as well as the local prosecutor, should form a team to develop a process that works for everyone. The law enforcement agencies and prosecutor should work to identify the specific areas of concern regarding the release of medical information, so that these areas can be addressed before an issue arises. The team leaders need to then repeat this process with private ambulance services and with the fire department paramedics and EMTs, if necessary.

Once the process has been developed, the risk managers need to train their respective teams on the process to ensure that no confusion remains. Part of the policy should include an escalation path if an issue does arise.

Glossary

agency	Governmental entity or organization that has specific responsibilities in the community.
Amber Alert	Federal legislation that requires the states to establish a plan for issuing alerts for missing persons, particularly children.
apprehension	Arrest of a suspect.
Bill of Rights	The first 10 amendments to the U.S. Constitution.
central figure in charge	Person in charge of an agency, usually the Chief of Police or Sheriff.
certification	The process of signing off on an officer's training for a particular policy. Both the officer and the trainer sign the certification.
civilian	Any person who does not work for a law enforcement entity.
common law	That which derives its force and authority from the universal consent and immemorial practice of the people. The system of jurisprudence that originated in England and which was later adopted in the U.S. that is based on precedent instead of statutory laws. (www.lectlaw.com, 2002)
constitutional deprivation	The act of violating an individual's constitutional rights.

constitutional limitations	The boundaries of what is covered under constitutional law.
counseling	Psychological or psychiatric assistance. Such assistance is often provided after a traumatic incident.
deadly force	Any force used by an officer that has a reasonable probability of causing death. (MML, 2003)
debriefing	Meeting held after an incident to discuss how the incident went. The purpose of the meeting is to apply lessons learned to future incidents.
deliberate indifference	The conscious or reckless disregard of the consequences of one's acts or omissions. (www.lectlaw.com, 2002)
deposition	The sworn testimony of a witness taken before trial held out of court with no judge present. The witness is placed under oath to tell the truth and lawyers for each party may ask questions. The questions and answers are recorded. When a person is unavailable to testify at trial, the deposition of that person may be used. Part of the pre-trial discovery (fact-finding) process. (www.lectlaw.com, 2002)
discipline	The act of correcting or punishing an individual for violating an agency's policies.
document repository	Central storage location for all documentation related to policy development.

documentation	Written information and other materials that describe policies, procedures, activities, and so on.
expert witness	A person with specialized training in a particular field who is called to assist either the plaintiff or defendent during litigation.
feedback	The transmission of evaluative or corrective information to the original or controlling source about an action, event, or process. (www.merrriam-webster.com, 2004)
first aid	Emergency care or treatment given to an ill or injured person before regular medical aid can be obtained. (www.merrriam-webster.com, 2004)
functional group	Set of individuals who have a similar skill set and job responsibilities. For example, line officers comprise a single functional group.
HIPAA	Health Insurance Portability and Accountability Act.
incident	A reportable event.
interjurisdictional matters	Situations, issues, or events that involve multiple law enforcement agencies.
jargon	Technical terminology specific to a particular group or activity.
judgment	The court's official decision about a matter presented to it.

law enforcement	An agency or individual responsible for enforcing the laws, ensuring public safety, and maintaining order in the community.
LEAF	Law Enforcement Action Forum. A statewide Michigan organization that helps law enforcement agencies develop effective policies and provides a forum to discuss issues.
learning style	The set of cognitive, emotional, characteristic and physiological factors that serve as relatively stable indicators of how a learner perceives, interacts with, and responds to the learning environment. (Keefe, 1979)
liability	Any legal responsibility, duty or obligation. The state of one who is bound in law and justice to do something which may be enforced by action. This liability may arise from contracts either express or implied or in consequence of torts committed. (www.lectlaw.com, 2002)
line officer	A sworn police officer in a non-supervisory position who works primarily on the street and with the community.
litigation	A case, controversy, or lawsuit. A contest authorized by law, in a court of justice, for the purpose of enforcing a right. (www.lectlaw.com, 2002)

Defensible Policies

Miranda warning	Statement that law enforcement uses to inform a suspect of his or her right to silence and to counsel. This warning arose from case law where charges were thrown out because the defendent did not understand his rights.
MML	Michigan Municipal League.
negligence	The failure to use reasonable care. The doing of something which a reasonably prudent person would not do, or the failure to do something which a reasonably prudent person would do under like circumstances. A departure from what an ordinary reasonable member of the community would do in the same community. (www.lectlaw.com, 2002)
policy	A set of guidelines that governs an individual's or agency's activities.
policy statement	The section of a policy that explains why the policy is needed for a particular area.
post-incident review	Meeting between the supervisor and officers involved in a reportable event. This meeting is intended to evaluate the incident and the policy governing the incident to ensure best practices and continuous learning.
procedure	A set of instructions for performing a task.
process	A set of activities that accomplishes a goal or task.

reasonableness	Standard of showing sound judgment and effort.
resource group	Cross-functional team that meets to develop policies.
respondeat superior	Legal doctrine that makes the person or agency in charge responsible for those acting under him or her.
risk manager	Person who is responsible for mitigating the risk of incidents and lawsuits. This person is a logical choice for managing the policy development group.
settlement	The act of resolving a lawsuit without a trial. Settlements often involve the payment of compensation by one party in satisfaction of the other party's claims.
statutes	Laws created by a legislative entity, such as Congress or the state legislature.
statutory protection	Activity protected by law.
statutory reference	Section of a policy that documents the law upon which the policy is based.
street reality	Actual events and incidents that occur in the community.
supervisor	Person who manages line officers and is responsible for providing them with training and direction.
target audience	Group or groups of people for whom a document is intended.

template	Electronic file that provides a format and outline for a document. Using a template improves consistency and helps to ensure that you don't leave out required elements.
testimony	The statement made by a witness under oath or affirmation. (www.lect-law.com, 2002)
training	The act of teaching an individual or group of individuals a new skill.
use of force	The attempt by an officer to establish control of a suspect by physical means when the suspect is resisting. (MML, 2002)

References

Champion, D.H. and Hooper, M.K. (downloaded 2004) *Introduction to American Policing: Section 7.3– Problem Solving.* www2.lc.cc.il.us/business/crmj/ 133ppts/ch7/AP7_3.ppt

Felder, R.M., et al. *Index to Learning Styles.* (2004) North Carolina State University. www.ncsu.edu/felder-public/ILSpage.html.

Keefe, J.W. (1979) 'Learning Style: An Overview'. In *NASSP's Student Learning Styles: Diagnosing and Prescribing Programs.* Reston, VA: National Association of Secondary School Principals, 1–17.

'Lectric Law Library's Legal Lexicon Lyceum. (2002) www.lectlaw.com/def.htm.

Merriam-Webster Online. (2004) www.Merriam-Webster.com. Merriam-Webster, Incorporated.

Rose, Colin. (1987) *Accelerated Learning.* New York: Dell, Inc. (re-issued).

Index